umami
THE FIFTH TASTE

umami
THE FIFTH TASTE

FOREWORDS BY Thomas Keller AND Harold McGee
INTRODUCTION BY Yoshihiro Murata

PHOTOGRAPHS BY Akira Saito

JAPAN PUBLICATIONS TRADING CO., LTD.

Edited by Dai-ichi Tsushinsha, Inc.

Published by Japan Publications Trading Co., Ltd.
1-2-1 Sarugaku-cho, Chiyoda-ku, Tokyo, 101-0064 Japan

DISTRIBUTORS
United States: Kodansha USA, Inc. through Oxford University Press,
198 Madison Avenue, New York, NY 10016.
Canada: Fitzhenry & Whiteside Ltd.,
195 Allstate Parkway, Markham,Ontario, L3R 4T8
United Kingdom, Ireland, continental Europe, Africa and the Middle East: Kodansha Europe Ltd.
40 Stockwell Street, Greenwich, London SE10 8EY
Asia and other countries: Japan Publications Trading Co., Ltd.
1-2-1 Sarugaku-cho, Chiyoda-ku, Tokyo, 101-0064 Japan

First Edition, 2014
23 22 21 20 19 18 17 16 15 14 10 9 8 7 6 5 4 3 2 1

ISBN 978-4-88996-391-5

CONTENTS

Umami is a universal taste, and although Japanese cooking has codified the term, chefs across cultures understand the balance and depth it brings to a dish. There is a cultural connection among chefs, one that crosses ethnic boundaries and language barriers, and this book is a perfect example of that connection.

In a discussion of umami in their worlds, some of the finest chefs introduce us to the fifth taste through anecdotes and recipes. Heston Blumenthal challenges our sense of taste and sound with a scallop dish featuring birch syrup, bergamont and coral royale. Peru's Virgilio Martinez recalls "meeting" umami at the age of ten and showcases the ingredients of his country from amaranth to yams cultivated on the Andean plateau.

Umami stays on the palate longer than any other taste, and just as that savory sweetness lingers, the memories, recipes and stories of this book will stay with you.

© Deborah Jones

Thomas Keller, The French Laundry

© Karl Petzke

I've been writing about foods and flavors for nearly forty years, and forty years ago, the term *umami* was unknown in the West except among a handful of experts in taste physiology. These experts knew it as a Japanese term for the taste sensation caused by monosodium glutamate (MSG) and a few other chemical compounds, but they disagreed as to whether the sensation amounted to an enhancement of the four known "basic" tastes, or was a distinct taste of its own. Meanwhile MSG itself had become widely known in the late 1960s and 1970s as the purported cause of the "Chinese restaurant syndrome," a cluster of uncomfortable and temporary sensations reported by some diners. In the 1984 first edition of my book *On Food & Cooking: The Science & Lore of the Kitchen*, I included MSG as a taste additive in foods that could affect sensitive people, and said that its actual taste effects were "mysterious."

The sciences—and cooking—have marched on. Over the ensuing decades, dozens of studies have demonstrated MSG's innocuousness in foods, and its ubiquity in foods that we especially value for their rich flavor. Biologists have demonstrated that we have taste receptors and nerve circuits dedicated to detecting MSG, pretty much clinching the case that umami is indeed a basic, universal taste of its own, not just a modifier of the other tastes. And so I was happy to be able to update my account of MSG and umami in the revised 2004 edition of my book, and delighted to participate in a 2008 symposium of scientists and chefs in San Francisco that celebrated the centenary of Kikunae Ikeda's discovery of umami taste. And I continue to watch with great interest as professional cooks and food lovers all over the world discover umami for themselves, and use that discovery to cook more effectively and get more pleasure from the experience of eating and drinking.

This book is the latest chapter in the story of umami, an intriguing mix of chemistry, sensory psychology, and reflections and recipes from leading chefs working all over the world. Umami is by no means the only key to deliciousness, and it remains somewhat mysterious—it's a more complex sensation than the other tastes, and seems to depend on them to be fully appreciated. But as the following pages make clear, an acquaintance with umami has become essential for the modern professional cook, and for anyone who wants to enjoy food to the fullest.

Harold McGee

INTRODUCTION

Over the past ten years the Japanese word "umami" has come to be known widely around the world. I have worked for many years as a Japanese chef with an eye on international cuisine, but I have never seen anything like the speed and extent of this term's spread.

A key factor behind this is the global rise of interest in healthy eating. At Kikunoi, my restaurant in Kyoto, we serve *kaiseki*, an elaborate meal of twelve to fourteen courses, but the entire meal, including dessert, comes to only about 1300 kilocalories. Chefs from other cuisines find this remarkable, but by going light on butter and oil and making good use of umami, we are able to produce a satisfying meal even with a low calorie count.

In 2004 we established the Japanese Culinary Academy as an incorporated non-profit organization to promote understanding and development of Japanese cuisine. One of the academy's activities is to invite chefs from overseas to come to Japan and learn about Japanese cuisine in special seminars. The program features a full schedule, extending from early in the morning to late in the evening, and includes a wide variety of experiences: Participants can listen to a farmer describe his work as they tour his fields; they can learn how to marinate fish from a fisherman who delivers seafood directly to *kaiseki* restaurants like Kikunoi; and they may even meet a professional knife sharpener and see how he keeps kitchen knives finely honed. The aim is to give the participants diverse perspectives on how Japanese food is prepared. On the final day of the program, the chefs all prepare Japanese dishes. A large group of judges tastes their creations, and the judges share their opinions with each of the chefs. Through this program the participants pick up the techniques of handling the ingredients of Japanese cuisine and drawing on their umami.

One can sense umami even without knowing about it by name. At a seminar I conducted overseas, I started out by having the three hundred participants taste *kombu* dashi. Hardly any of them could distinguish between the dashi and plain water. Next, I had them taste the dashi with some shaved *katsuobushi* (dried bonito flakes) on their tongues. About half were able to taste the difference. Finally, I added salt and soy sauce to the dashi. Almost all the tasters pronounced the result delicious. This step-by-

step approach allows people to understand what umami is and how it can be sensed.

I think of umami as being something like the "tote bag" of tastes. The other four basic tastes (sweet, sour, salty, bitter) can all fit inside this bag. It does not mask the other tastes but wraps each of them gently and creates harmony among them. Umami is central to Japanese cuisine, but the key point is to achieve a pleasing balance among the five basic tastes.

"Umami" is a Japanese word, and the taste was originally identified by a Japanese scientist, but it has been used in cuisines around the world for centuries by people with no knowledge of the word or of *dashi*, the umami-rich stock used in Japanese cuisine. Examples include Russia's beet stock, made with beets and beef, Britain's Marmite and vegetable soup, and China's *shang tang* made with *Jinhua* ham. Chicken breasts, dried tomatoes, and morel mushrooms can also be used to make stock. Now that chefs have learned about umami, they are actively using it in their cuisine, and health-conscious diners have also picked up on this taste, promoting its spread to tables around the world.

The ingredients of good food know no borders. But good cooking also requires communication. We Japanese chefs have been picking up hints from the cuisines of other countries, such as China and France. And non-Japanese chefs have been adopting practices from Japan, including the use of dashi and of umami. The world surely has many more umami-rich foodstuffs waiting to be discovered. As a chef, I am eager to try out diverse ingredients. And I am also eager to share Japan's splendid techniques, such as the use of umami and dashi to bring out the best from ingredients of all sorts—techniques that can present wonderful new possibilities for cuisines of every genre.

The science of savory

Umami taste and food preferences

John Prescott, Ph.D.

TasteMatters Research & Consulting
www.taste-matters.org

Our sense of taste arises from the contact of chemical compounds, including those in foods, with taste receptors that are located mostly within the taste buds on the tongue. Traditionally—in fact, as far back as Aristotle—sweetness, saltiness, sourness and bitterness have been recognized as fundamental in all foods and drinks. Of course, these qualities are insufficient to describe our experiences from eating foods. Compared to the rich inventory of thousands of different odors that contribute to the flavors in our diet, the range of taste qualities seems remarkably limited.[1]

Being responsive to a small set of basic tastes does suggest that each of the qualities must be significant in some way. Why have we evolved to be sensitive to these qualities specifically? As Brillat-Savarin noted in his gastronomical meditations published in 1825, taste can be reduced "in the last analysis, into two expressions, agreeable or disagreeable."[2] In contrast to our preferences for odors/flavors, which are molded by exposure and learning from an early age, preferences for pure tastes are remarkably fixed. Distinct, and unambiguous, facial expressions to sweetness and bitterness are present at birth in humans, monkeys, and rats, and are essentially the same responses that we have as adults (see Fig 1). Both in terms of willingness to ingest, and also in the quality of these characteristic facial expressions, sweetness is highly liked and bitterness rejected in human neonates.[3,4] Sourness is also disliked, especially at high levels. A preference for saltiness, on the other hand, develops in the first few post-natal months.[5] Liking for pure tastes also seems to be relatively independent of culture or diet. Comparisons between cultures whose diets are very different, such as Japan, Taiwan and Australia, have found remarkably similar patterns of likes and dislikes for basic tastes.[6]

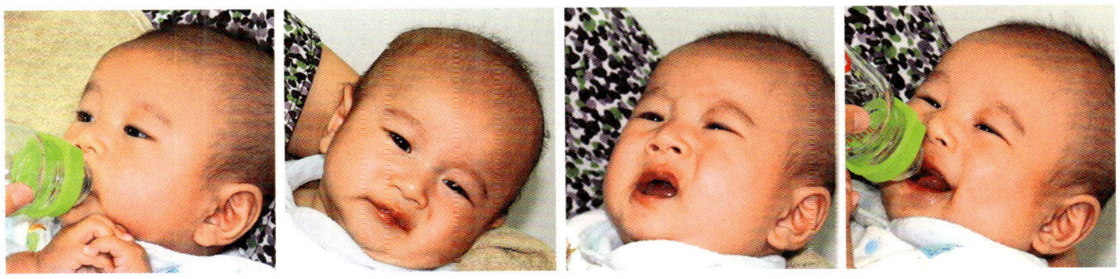

sweet | sour | bitter | umami

Fig 1 These photos show the reactions of a baby (a four-month-old boy) after tasting sweet (10% sucrose solution), sour (lemon juice), bitter (bitter melon juice) and vegetable bouillon with 0.1% MSG. The presence of such characteristic expressions shortly after birth strongly suggests that our responses to basic tastes such as sweet, sour, bitter and umami are innate.

Photos Umami Information Center.

The explanation for innate responses to taste qualities lies in their ability to signal nutrients and toxins. Thus, the palatability of sweetness is thought to signal the presence of energy in the form of calories provided by sugars and other plant carbohydrates, which are crucial to survival. Consistent with this interpretation, animals such as cats that are solely carnivores are indifferent to sweetness. Saltiness signals the presence of the sodium ion (Na^+), crucial for maintaining the body's fluid balance. The strong dislike that we naturally have to bitterness is thought to be a protective mechanism. Many plants manufacture toxins as a defense against predators, and many of these toxins are bitter. The significance of our dislike for high levels of sourness is not as clear-cut. It may be a signal for unripeness/spoilage in foods, or the fact that concentrated, and thus extremely sour, acids can cause tissue damage. Hence, one way of looking at our sense of taste is that it is a "gatekeeper" between the external environment and the internal environment of our body whose function is to ensure that ingested substances maximize our survival.

In addition to these four well-known qualities, we now recognize the existence of another basic taste. In the early twentieth century, a Japanese scientist, Kikunae Ikeda, first synthesized glutamate from the seaweed *kombu*, commonly used as a soup base in Japanese cuisine. He used the term *umami* to describe the quality that glutamate produced when added to savory foods. Ikeda described umami as the "peculiar taste which we feel as '*umai*' [meaning brothy, meaty, or savory], arising from fish, meat and so forth."[7] The Japanese word umami, translated approximately as "savory deliciousness," refers to the quality of foods containing significant amounts of naturally-occurring glutamate (a derivative of glutamic acid, a non-essential amino acid), its sodium salt, monosodium glutamate (MSG), or 5'-ribonucleotides such as guanosine monophosphate (GMP) and inosine monophosphate (IMP). Ikeda was convinced that umami represented a new, distinct taste. However, it is only during the past two decades that there has come to be a general agreement with Ikeda's proposition from within the scientific taste community. A considerable amount of recent research has shown that the way in which umami is perceived and the biological processes underlying this perception are unique to glutamate/glutamic acid, its compounds, and ribonucleotides.

What is umami?

What is the taste of umami? Glutamate as a separate taste outside of food, dissolved in water, is not particularly palatable, and it is hard to define its quality. It is often described as "mouth-filling," suggesting a texture. One of the common forms of glutamate, the flavor-enhancer mono-sodium glutamate (MSG), is somewhat salty (because of the sodium component), but it also has an additional quality. In human-behavioral studies of umami, when subjects are asked to sort a selection of taste substances into groups based on similarity, substances with an umami quality are shown to be very different from other taste qualities.[8] Behavioural and physiological studies with animals also point to umami as a distinct taste. Thus, there are taste nerve fibers in the tongue, as well as neurons in the brain, that respond more strongly to MSG than to other taste substances. Most important, though, has been the discovery of a receptor in rodent taste buds that responds only to umami.[9] As with similar receptors for sweet and bitter, umami receptors are the molecular mechanisms present in taste buds that convert a chemical signal into a specific electrical code that is transmitted to the taste areas of the brain.

From the point of view of our own food experiences, though, we are all intimately familiar with umami even if the word itself is relatively novel. Every cuisine has a concept of savoriness, often seen to be synonymous with "meatiness." We can recognize, for example, savory (non-sweet) foods that are more or less rich-tasting, and this quality is primarily determined by the presence of umami compounds. The preparation of a pasta sauce from basic ingredients such as onions, carrots, celery, tomatoes, mushrooms, chicken stock and Parmesan cheese is fundamentally an exercise in getting umami to our taste buds. What each of these ingredients possesses is glutamate or ribonucleotides in relatively high levels. Parmesan cheese, for example, is estimated to be about 1% glutamate. Many Asian cultures increase the umami quality of their cuisines through sauces based on fermented vegetables or fish. Soy sauce and the fish sauces of Vietnam and Thailand are examples. Sauces based on fermented anchovies, such as Worcestershire sauce, are also popular in Western cuisines. A Roman equivalent of fish sauce, *garum*, was being used 2,000 years ago as a way of enhancing food flavors. In cooking generally, the effect of adding umami compounds is an increase in savoriness, richness and an almost tactile mouth-filling quality. Mostly, this is achieved by the addition of common ingredients in soups, sauces and stews such as glutamate-rich vegetables and meats.

As with other taste qualities, it appears that our response to umami taste is innate. Breast milk is both sweet and high in glutamate, both of which may contribute to its universal acceptance. Newborns show facial responses to clear vegetable soup indicative of dislike—pursed lips, gaping mouth and wrinkled nose. However, when MSG is added to the same soup, the infants respond with facial expressions similar to those seen with liked sweet tastes, including licking, mouthing and sucking.[10] Recent research has shown that preference for glutamate is highly dependent on its context—in essence, it becomes highly liked when part of an overall flavor.[11] This, of course, is true for different tastes in many contexts. Bitterness as a quality is universally disliked, but when part of the flavor of beer and coffee produces the two most preferred beverages worldwide.

About MSG

The acceptance of MSG in food for neonates is typical of the impact of glutamate in foods generally. It is well known that the addition of glutamate to suitable foods produces an increase in the acceptability for the sensory properties of those foods.[12, 13] Thus, one study found that a soup in which MSG was increased by 20% was judged as more savory, satisfying and pleasant.[14] Increases in food acceptability are clearly mediated by changes in the sensory properties of the foods produced by added MSG. Fig. 2 (see p. 14) shows changes in qualities such as richness and saltiness as well as acceptability of three common foods.

Although adding MSG to a food does influence its saltiness, it is clear that the effects on other sensory properties and on palatability are not just an effect of salt on flavor. For example, if one equates the amount of sodium in two products of the same type, the one that contains the added glutamate will always be preferred.[15] Alternatively, other glutamate compounds, such as calcium glutamate, do not add saltiness but still increase the palatability of foods to which it is added.[16]

What underlies the apparently universal increase in palatability produced by umami tastes? As noted above, it has been suggested that sweetness is highly liked because the body values the energy that it signals. The same argument is used to explain the impact of fat in foods on palatability (in fact, there is recent evidence for the existence of an oral fat "taste" receptor). If umami is also a basic taste quality, the positive impact of glutamate in foods may reflect the body's use of the glutamate for some essential purpose. Since the body produces a sufficient quantity of glutamate necessary for the metabolic processes in which it is involved,[17] glutamate is itself not required from dietary sources. It has been suggested, therefore, that the palatability of glutamate may mean that it is a marker or signal for some other nutrient with which it is reliably associated. In turn, its effect on palatability facilitates consumption of that nutrient. The most obvious candidate is protein, since glutamic acid is an amino acid present in proteins that we consume.

This idea has appeal but has been difficult to prove. Because the body manufactures most of its own glutamate, we cannot show the effects of glutamate deficiency in the way that deficiency can be shown for salt, for example. Nevertheless, there have been studies showing that people with very low protein intakes prefer higher concentrations of glutamate than those whose protein intake is adequate.[18] However, this doesn't explain why glutamate increases food palatability irrespective of whether our protein intake is adequate or not. An alternative idea to explain the palatability effect of glutamate comes from evidence that dietary glutamate is involved in crucial metabolic processes within the body, possibly even being used by the body as an energy source for such processes in the gut.[17]

Regardless of the actual underlying physiology, there are good reasons to believe that our preference for umami reflects the value that the body places on the glutamate that we ingest in foods. Firstly, in common with sucrose (but neither water nor salt), the taste of MSG can trigger increases in the pancreatic secretions that signal the body's preparation for energy intake.[19] Another way of demonstrating the value of ingested glutamate has been to show how it can produce a liking for flavors with which it is paired. Studies using dietary energy sources such as sugar or fat have shown that associated novel flavors become highly liked following repeated pairing, especially when the energy source is ingested, rather than merely tasted.[20] The interpretation of these effects is that the flavor associated with sugar or fat is a signal to the body that energy is to follow, and so preference for the flavor is a motivation to ingest it. This is supported by the fact that these pairings only reliably produce liked flavors when the pairings take place while the person (or animal) is hungry—that is, when the body actually

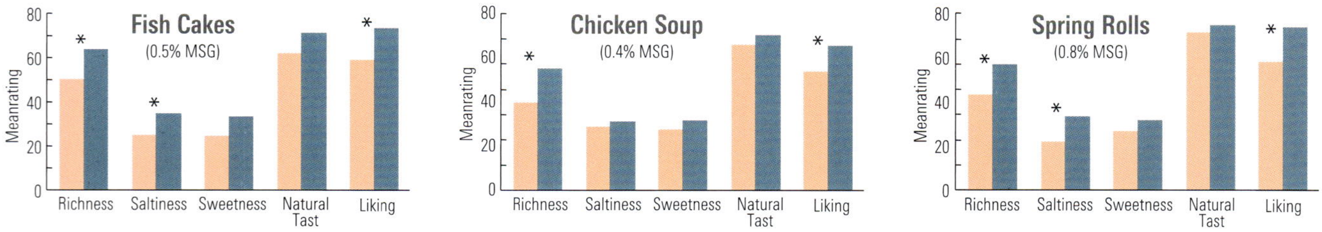

Fig 2 Effects of adding MSG (dark bars) to three savory foods on ratings of *liking, richness, sweetness, saltiness* and *natural taste*. (* indicates significant increase in ratings by adding MSG)

needs the energy. In fact, the same effect has been shown using novel flavors paired with ingested glutamate, which become liked to a greater extent than if the pairing takes place without subsequent ingestion, for example, by simply having the flavor and glutamate repeatedly tasted together.[21] In other words, the body places some value on the ingested glutamate. Whether that value is as an energy source—by analogy with similar effects shown with sucrose or fat—is still not certain.

The recognition and role of umami

The role of umami as a basic taste should perhaps also be seen in a wider context. The recognition of umami as a basic taste quality produced by glutamate and ribonucleotides may be only one example of the responsiveness of the taste system to amino acids generally. The taste system may be both more broadly receptive and more flexible when it comes to biologically important compounds. As one example, animals fed a diet deficient in just one essential amino acid will recognize its presence in foods, consuming those foods preferentially.[22] This suggests that the taste system is responsive to metabolic needs to the extent that it can create a temporary "basic taste" by becoming sensitive to a required nutrient to fulfill the need. Similarly, studies of malnourished children have shown the addition of an otherwise unpalatable amino acid mixture can increase the consumption of a soup,[23] suggesting increased palatability. These effects disappeared when the nutritional state returned to normal. Glutamate, by contrast, improved the palatability of the soup in these subjects, but this effect was not responsive to nutritional state, a fact in keeping with its status as a non-essential amino acid.

Understanding our preferences for tastes in foods, and the role that they play in promoting flavor preferences, is crucial to recognizing our motivations for food choices and, of course, the health consequences of our diets. This applies particularly to the role played by umami tastes since, unlike sugars and fats, they are preferred without contributing to obesity or other health problems.

One way in which umami compounds may help provide healthier foods is through substitution for either fat or salt. Since savory foods are a major source of dietary fat, the use of umami to compensate for the loss of richness experienced when animal fats are reduced is a distinct possibility. But one area in which substitution has been studied extensively is the use of MSG as a salt replacer. Dietary sodium is a major contributor to high blood pressure and its consequences. There is a general agreement among health professionals and, increasingly, government health agencies that sodium reduction is a positive step. Since most of the sodium added to foods is for taste alone, MSG provides a possible alternative. Although MSG itself contains sodium, it is at a lower proportion than table salt. However, salt is primarily added not to produce overt "saltiness" but to boost flavor, the same reason that MSG is also added to foods. In fact, it has been shown that adding MSG to soups maintains their flavor acceptability when the salt level has been reduced.[24, 25]

One issue often raised when considering MSG as a food additive is the negative attitudes that some consumers have about its use. While, from a health perspective, these concerns are baseless, the beliefs have been pervasive. A few years ago, though, I tested the preferences for soup in a group of consumers who had such negative beliefs. They were given soups either with or without added MSG and their preferences were clear—they preferred the added MSG version. The research had another aspect however. We manipulated the labels on the soup—some showed "contains added MSG," while others showed "no added MSG," but independently of the actual soup content. So some soups had accurate labels, and some did not. In any case, the labels had no effect in this group—the MSG-containing soup was preferred, despite the consumers' negative attitudes.[26]

As noted above, most food-related health questions currently emphasize reductions—of salt, fat and sugar, primarily. However, in cases of impoverished diets, the concern may be how to ensure adequate food intake. Research on the role of umami in foods in this context has examined its ability not merely to improve food flavors (although this is a part of the issue) but also in its ability to stimulate appetite and motivation to eat. Further research on the ways in which glutamate can promote liking for flavors with which it is paired has shown that in addition to flavor preference increasing, subsequently tasting the flavor in a food increases overall appetite and the amount of that food that is consumed.[27] Here, the reaction to the flavor signal for glutamate increased motivation to eat. This is consistent with a demonstration that MSG added to novel foods increased the intake of those foods over a four-week period, relative to the same foods without added MSG.[12]

The practical implications of this have been explored in studies in which the ability of MSG to enhance palatability has been employed therapeutically to enhance food intake in elderly patients and improve their nutritional status as a result. These studies produced enhanced food satisfaction and energy intake, as well positive physical signs such as improved immune function, plasma protein levels and physical strength.[28, 29]

For the cuisines of the world

Umami is a key part of the cuisines of the world, regardless of where their proteins are sourced or how their savory foods are prepared. Some years ago, Elizabeth Rozin wrote *The Flavor Principle Cookbook*,[30] based on the research that she and psychologist husband Paul Rozin had undertaken on culinary themes and variations cross-culturally.[31] Their focus was on showing the combinations of ingredients that made each culture's cuisine unique and identifiable from the outside. They recognized too that part of the role of unique but familiar ingredients or cooking procedures was that they allowed the cuisine to expand if required to, say by a shortage of some key protein. That culture's flavor principle would allow substitutions of ingredients to be immediately acceptable, thus ensuring that the cuisine was flexible enough to respond to environmental changes. Otherwise, wrote Paul Rozin, widespread food neophobia towards new ingredients could potentially compromise a population's health.

While the Rozins' focus was on flavor ingredients that distinguished food cultures, we can recognize too that there are some universal qualities that signal the appropriateness of a substance for consumption irrespective of geography. As noted earlier, one of these universal flavor principles is sweetness, innately recognized as a source of energy; another is the physiologically vital saltiness. To sweetness and saltiness, we can also add umami. In the context of cuisines, umami is a universal flavor principle that underlies and unites savory foods in all cultures.

REFERENCES

1. J. Prescott, *Taste Matters: Why we like the foods we do* (London: Reaktion Books, 2012).
2. J.-A.Brillat-Savarin, *The Physiology of Taste* (London: Penguin Books, 1825, 1994 ed. cited).
3. J.E. Steiner et al., "Comparative expression of hedonic impact: affective reactions to taste by human infants and other primates," *Neuroscience & Biobehavioral Reviews* 25, no. 1 (2001): 53–74.
4. J.A. Desor, O. Maller, and R.E. Turner, "Taste in acceptance of sugars by human infants," *Journal of Comparative and Physiological Psychology* 84, no. 3 (1973): 496–501.
5. G.K. Beauchamp, B. Cowart, and H.J. Schmidt, "Development of Chemosensory Sensitivity and Preference," in *Smell and Taste in Health and Disease*, ed. T.V. Getchell et al. (New York: Raven Press, 1991), 405–16.
6. J. Prescott, "Comparisons of taste perceptions and preferences of Japanese and Australian consumers: overview and implications for cross-cultural sensory research," *Food Quality and Preference* 9, no. 6 (1998): 393–402.
7. K. Ikeda, "New Seasonings," *Chemical Senses* 97, no. 9 (2002): 847–49.
8. S. Yamaguchi, "Fundamental properties of umami in human taste sensation," in *Umami: A Basic Taste*, ed. Y. Kawamura and M.R. Kare (New York: Marcel Dekker, Inc., 1987), 41–73.
9. N. Chaudhari, A.M. Landin, and S.D. Roper, "A metabotropic glutamate receptor variant functions as a taste receptor," *Nature Neuroscience* 3, no. 2 (2000): 113–19.
10. J.E. Steiner, "What the human neonate can tell us about umami," in *Umami: A Basic Taste*, ed. Y. Kawamura and M.R. Kare (New York: Marcel Dekker, Inc., 1987), 97–123.
11. E.T. Rolls, "Functional neuroimaging of umami taste: what makes umami pleasant?" *American Journal of Clinical Nutrition* 90, suppl. (2009): 804S–13S.
12. F. Bellisle et al., "Monosodium glutamate as a palatability enhancer in the European diet," *Physiology & Behavior* 49, no. 5 (1991): 869–74.
13. S. Yamaguchi, "Basic properties of umami and effects on humans," *Physiol. Behav.* 49, no. 5 (1991): 833–41.
14. P.J. Rogers and J. Blundell, "Umami and appetite: Effects of monosodium glutamate on hunger and food intake in human subjects," *Physiol. Behav*. 48 (1990): 801–04.
15. A. Okiyama and G.K. Beauchamp, "Taste dimensions of monosodium glutamate (MSG) in a food system: Role of glutamate in young American subjects," *Physiol. Behav.* 65, no. 1 (1998): 177–81.
16. F. Bellisle, A.M. Dartois, and M. Broyer, "Two studies on the acceptability of calcium glutamate as a potassium-free sodium substitute in children," *Journal of Renal Nutrition* 2, no. 3 (1992): 42–46.
17. P.J. Reeds et al., "Intestinal glutamate metabolism," *Journal of Nutrition* 130 (2000): 978S–82S.
18. C. Murphy, "Flavor preference for monosodium glutamate and casein hydrolysate in young and elderly persons," in *Umami: A Basic Taste*, ed. Y. Kawamura and M.R. Kare (New York: Marcel Dekker, Inc., 1987), 139–51.
19. M. Naim et al., "Interaction of MSG taste with nutrition: Perspectives in consummatory behavior and digestion," *Physiol. Behav.* 49 (1991): 1019–24.
20. D.L. Kern et al., "The postingestive consequences of fat condition preferences for flavors associated with high dietary fat," *Physiol. Behav.* 54 (1993): 71–76.
21. J. Prescott, "Effects of added glutamate on liking for novel food flavors," *Appetite* 42, no. 2 (2004): 143–50.
22. M. Mori et al., "Taste preference and protein nutrition and L-amino acid homeostasis in male Sprague-Dawley rats," *Physiol. Behav.* 49, no. 5 (1991): 987–96.
23. G.K. Beauchamp, M. Vazquez de Vaquera, and P.B. Pearson, "Dietary status of human infants and their sensory responses to amino acid flavour," in *Umami: A Basic Taste*, ed. Y. Kawamura and M.R. Kare (New York: Marcel Dekker, Inc., 1987), 125–138.
24. K. Roininen, L. Lahteenmaki, and H. Tuorila, "Effect of Umami taste on pleasantness of low-salt soups during repeated testing," *Physiol. Behav.* 60, no. 3 (1996): 953–58.
25. H. Tuorila, U. Hellemann, and I. Matuszewska, "Can sodium contents of foods be reduced by adding flavors? Studies with beef broth," *Physiol. Behav.* 47 (1990): 709–12.
26. J. Prescott and A. Young, "Does information about MSG (monosodium glutamate) content influence consumer ratings of soups with and without added MSG?" *Appetite* 39 (2002): 25–33.
27. M.R. Yeomans et al., "Acquired flavor acceptance and intake facilitated by monosodium glutamate in humans," *Physiol. Behav.* 93 (2008): 958–66.
28. S.S. Schiffman, "Sensory enhancement of foods for the elderly with monosodium glutamate," *Food Reviews International* 14, no. 2/3 (1998): 321–34.
29. S.S. Schiffman and Z.S. Warwick, "Use of flavour amplified foods to improve nutritional status in elderly persons," in *Nutrition and Chemical Senses in Aging: Recent Advances and Current Research Needs, Annals of the New York Academy of Sciences,* Vol. 561, ed. C. Murphy, W.S. Cain, and D.M. Hegsted (New York: The New York Academy of Sciences, 1989), 267–276.
30. E. Rozin, *Ethnic Cuisine: The Flavor-Principle Cookbook* (Brattleboro: The Stephen Greene Press, 1983).
31. E. Rozin and P. Rozin, "Culinary themes and variations," *Journal of Natural History* 90, no. 2 (1981): 6–14.

EU

HESTON BLUMENTHAL

The Fat Duck Bray

ROPE

ALEXANDRE BOURDAS

SaQuaNa Honfleur

HESTON BLU

Although umami can be used to enhance the taste of some foods, it is only one of the five classified taste components. The others should not be dismissed as any less important than umami. However, an understanding of umami does help with the blend and balance of the different tastes. Chefs always put salt first when thinking about taste, but other tastes, notably acidity and bitterness, must never be forgotten, as they can add essential backbone to savory dishes.

© Neal Haynes

My first surprising umami experience, one that really knocked me for six, occurred while eating a cold, cooked sea snail as part of a *plateau de fruits de la mer* at a fish restaurant in Montpellier, France in the 1980s. How can I describe the experience? As I ate it, I got a massive hit—an extremely pleasant fullness of taste that filled my mouth and also seemed to hit every part of my tongue, gums and roof of my mouth. It was a sensation that was surprising, unexpected but totally delicious.

To showcase umami to those who had not experienced it before, I deliberately and intentionally created a dish that I called "Umami Broth," which was absolutely full of many umami tastes. I included a lot of different umami ingredients: *kombu*, soy sauce, white saury, dried shiitake mushrooms, lightly poached mackerel, and of course tomatoes, amongst other things.

When making this broth, which was based on tomatoes, I decided to look at the three key parts of a tomato and their umami content. I compared the umami taste in the skin to the flesh, and the pulp with the seeds. To my surprise I felt that the very part of the tomato that classical French cooking told you to throw away, the seeds and pulp, had the biggest "mouth feel."

We had been doing a lot of work with Don Mottram and his team at Reading University and learning a lot from them about taste and flavor. So I spoke to him about this, and we realized that, through our conversation, it was something

SOUND OF THE SEA

RECIPE P. 22

MENTHAL

that had never been looked at before. This led to one of my early research papers, which proved that the very part of the tomato that classical French cooking tells you to throw away is the bit that contributes the biggest taste.*

Something similar happened with sherry. I became an ambassador for the Sherry Institute, as I had been a big fan of this wine for a long time. I felt that it was under-rated as a drink and found that there was something in sherry that regular wine didn't have. It had an intense mouth feel that almost reminded me of umami. Therefore, as with my tomato experiments, I contacted Don, and this resulted in further research that is currently being published as a paper. It turned out that sherry contained dipeptides, which do not technically create an umami taste but can create a similar effect, an effect that regular wines cannot create.

On the subject of umami and its influence on the preparation of food and menu design, I am actively involved in another original and continuing umami research project with the Reading University team of Professor Mottram and Lisa Methven. This is in collaboration with the Royal Berkshire Regional Health Authority. The aim of this project is to utilize the taste enhancing properties of umami to improve the acceptability and palatability of food for elderly patients. From a health perspective, although elevated sodium levels present a recognized health concern, and we have to be careful with salt content, we can be much more flexible about glutamate. Therefore we are able to increase the amount of glutamate in Bolognese sauce preparations without affecting the salt content. We can also prepare more palatable food using natural umami-rich ingredients like Parmesan cheese and tomato.

* M-J. Oruna-Concha, L. Methven, H. Blumenthal, C. Young, D.S. Mottram, "Differences in Glutamic Acid and 5'-Ribonucleotide Contents between Flesh and Pulp of Tomatoes and the Relationship with Umami Taste," *J. Agric. Food Chem.* 55 (2007), 5776–5780.

Heston Blumenthal's recipes measure liquids by weight rather than volume for better accuracy. Many measures are in metric only; attempting to scale these ingredients using Imperial units may reduce precision and lead to recipe failure.

SOUND OF THE SEA

Sound can transform the flavor of a dish. Here cured mackerel, baby anchovies, *panko* breadcrumbs, bonito flakes, samphire, sea jelly beans, seared abalone and four sorts of seaweed are prepared and combined so that what you see is an edible version of the shore's edge—sand, sea-spume, and even the tide-mark. At the Fat Duck the dish is served with an iPod so that you also hear the sound of waves crashing and seagulls calling. The appeal to both senses in unison creates a powerful and emotional experience.

For the Ponzu

65 g sake
2 whole, fresh *yuzu* citrus
1 whole, fresh *sudachi* citrus
700 g mirin
525 g rice vinegar
550 g *tamari* soy sauce
110 g *usukuchi* soy sauce
10 g ($\frac{1}{3}$ oz.) dried bonito flakes
15 g ($\frac{1}{2}$ oz.) *Rishiri* kombu (dried), browned on both sides over an open flame

Pour the sake into a pan, bring to a boil over a high heat and flame off the alcohol. When the flames have died down, remove the pan from the heat and set aside to cool. Add all the remaining ingredients, place in an airtight container and refrigerate for one month.

Strain the liquid through a fine sieve lined with muslin that has been previously soaked in water, adjust the seasoning with tamari, usukuchi soy sauce or rice vinegar as necessary. Store in the fridge.

For the miso oil

1 kg ($2\frac{1}{4}$ lbs.) red miso
400 g (14 oz.) white miso
1 kg grape seed oil

Fold all the ingredients together very carefully, then cover and refrigerate for 48 hours. Gently strain through damp muslin to separate the top layer of oil from the heavier miso below, and reserve the oil.

For the Braised Shiroita Kombu

5 kg mineral water
800 g glucose syrup
100 sheets *shiroita* kombu
600 g mirin
850 g rice wine vinegar
250 g *usukuchi* soy sauce
30 g (1 oz.) sea salt

Combine the water and the glucose in a pot wide enough for the sheets of shiroita kombu to lie out flat, but not too wide for them to have room to float around during cooking (a 13 in./32 cm pot is ideal). Remove the shiroita kombu from the package and place the sheets one at a time into a separate container filled with cold water, lying flat, so that each sheet is facing the same direction.

Note: the sheets will be stuck together slightly and it is important for even cooking and marination that they be peeled off one at a time.

Remove each sheet, one at a time, and wipe the viscous fluid off of it. Place each sheet facing the same direction into the pot with the water and glucose.

Bring the pot to a low simmer and cover the surface of the kombu with a sheet of muslin to keep it submerged in the liquid, ensuring even cooking. Bring the water just to a simmer and set a timer for 20 minutes.

Simmer the kombu gently for 20 minutes and check doneness (the kombu should be cooked through while retaining texture). Gently transfer the kombu into a $\frac{1}{3}$ *gastronorm* pan so that the sheets are all facing the same direction, and cover with the reserved muslin from the cooking process.

Drain any liquid that has collected in the gastronorm pan back into the pot and reserve the kombu at room temperature.

Strain the liquid from the pot through a fine sieve into a container, rinse out the pot, and return the liquid to the pot.

Bring the remaining liquid in the

pot up to a boil, first skimming any impurities that have risen to the surface, and begin to reduce the liquid.

Meanwhile, heat the mirin in a saucepot and flame off the alcohol. Reduce the mirin by half and add to the reducing water mixture. Add the rice vinegar and reduce the mixture to a syrup. Remove from the heat and add the soy sauce and salt. Pour the hot liquid over the kombu.

Wrap the container in cling film and refrigerate for 24 hours. Check the consistency of the liquid as well as the acidity and seasoning. If further adjustments are required, drain the liquid into a saucepot and return to a simmer.

Pour the liquid back over the kombu and refrigerate for a further 24 hours before using.

For the Sound of the Sea Foam

For the Base

200 g (7 oz.) unsalted butter
400 g (14 oz.) shallots
40 g (1⅓ oz.) garlic
Scant ⅔ cup (140 ml) Noilly Prat
1½ cups (360 ml) white wine
4 L vegetable stock
8 L de-ionized water
90 g (3 oz.) kombu
520 g (17 oz.) *laitue de mer*
160 g (5 oz.) dried shiitake
60 g (2 oz.) parsley stalks

Heat the butter in a pan and gently sweat the shallots and garlic in the butter for 4 to 5 minutes. Add the Noilly Prat and the white wine and reduce to a syrup. Add the vegetable stock, water, kombu, laitue de mer, dried shiitake, and parsley stalks and bring up to 150°F (65°C). Hold at this temperature for 30 minutes.

Pass through a fine sieve lined with muslin that has been previously soaked in water and allow to cool. When cool, skim off any solidified butter and pass again.

For the Finished Sauce

1 L base
Scant 1 cup (200 ml) de-ionized water
¼ cup (65 ml) white soy sauce
7 g lecithin
6.6 g sodium caseinate
200 g (7 oz.) codium seaweed

Combine the base, water, white soy sauce, lecithin and sodium caseinate and heat gently (below 150°F/65°C).

Infuse with codium for 3 hours in the fridge.

For the "sand"

640 g (21 oz.) N-Zorbit tapioca maltodextrin
108.5 g (3½ oz.) blue shimmer powder
890 g (30 oz.) miso oil
7 g salt
200 g (7 oz.) crispy fried *panko* bread crumbs fried in grapeseed oil until golden brown and then lightly ground
35 g (1 oz.) chopped Grape-Nuts, fried
45 g (1½ oz.) *shirasu* (baby Japanese anchovies), fried in grapeseed oil until golden brown
20 g cod liver oil
7.5 g bonito *furikake* per 100 g sand

Combine the tapioca maltodextrin with the blue shimmer powder and mix well, add the miso oil gradually while whisking until the mix resembles sand. Season with sea salt, add panko, fold in well, and then the Grape-Nuts. Add the shirasu and cod liver oil and reserve in an airtight container. Just before serving, mix in 7.5 g bonito furikake per 100 g of the sand mix.

For the *Hijiki* Seaweed

150 g (5 oz.) dried *hijiki* seaweed
25 g *usukuchi* soy sauce
20 g mirin

Soak the hijiki in warm water until softened (about 5 minutes), drain off the water. Rinse with fresh water and drain again. Season with soy sauce and mirin. Cover and refrigerate until needed.

For the Codium Seaweed

Rinse the codium seaweed 3 times in cold water. Place in an 8% salt solution for 10 minutes. Remove from the brine, drain and refrigerate until needed.

For the Red *Tosaka* Seaweed

Rinse the tosaka seaweed 3 times in cold water, drain and refrigerate until needed.

For the Abalone

It is imperative that the abalones are kept as stress-free as possible during this entire process. To do this the water temperature must be kept between 54°F (12°C) and 59°F (15°C), the abalone must be kept in the dark, and the water needs to be aerated regularly (every 15 minutes with a whisk).

Prepare the following brine solutions

3.5% *Seamix* sea salt in water
2% *Seamix* sea salt in water
0.5% *Seamix* sea salt in water

Place the abalones into the 3.5% solution, cover and leave for a minimum of 30 minutes. Transfer the abalone from the 3.5% solution to the 2% solution, cover again and leave for 2 hours. After 2 hours the abalones should seem quite tired; they shouldn't push back when you touch or lift the skirt. Transfer the abalones from the 2% solution to the 0.5% solution, cover again and leave for another 2 hours.

Transfer the abalones from the 0.5% solution to a container with fresh cold water. After 2 hours begin checking to see if they are done. They should be easily removed from their shells with a spoon. This can take up to 4 hours.

Once removed from their shells, remove the mantle and other organs, and then cut out the head. Place the abalones in vacuum pack bags, 10 per bag, and store on ice until needed.

For the Yellow Tail

For the Cure
350 g (12 oz.) salt
100 g (3½ oz.) white caster sugar
12.5 g (½ oz.) lemon zest
22.5 g (⅔ oz.) bergamot zest

Yellow tail fillets

Panné the yellow tail with a generous amount of the cure. Place the fillet on a rack inside of a container, cover tightly and allow to stand in the fridge to cure for 15 minutes to 1 hour depending on size. Rinse under running cold water until all of the cure mix is removed and dry on all sides using paper towels. Slice and reserve in the fridge until needed.

For the Mackerel

For the Cure
400 g (14 oz.) salt
400 g (14 oz.) white caster sugar
20 g (⅔ oz.) lime zest
80 g (2½ oz.) lemon zest
25 g (⅔ oz.) coriander seeds

transglutaminase
mackerel filets

Place the coriander seeds in a food processor and blend to a fine powder. Mix with the sugar, salt, lemon zest and lime zest, sprinkle a layer into a shallow container, then place the mackerel fillets on it flesh-side down. Cover with clingfilm and refrigerate for 25 minutes. Rinse under cold running water and dry using paper towels.

Using a small fine sieve, sprinkle transglutaminase over the flesh of both fillets, then using a clean, dry pastry brush dust off as much excess as possible. Place a piece of clingfilm on a work surface. Lay 1 fillet on it skin-side down, then place the other fillet on top (flesh to flesh and nose to tail), making sure the flaps of trimmed skin overlap slightly. Together they should look like a trimmed, boneless fish. Carefully roll the clingfilm around the fish, then twist the ends—the fish should be tightly wrapped, but take care not to distort the shape of the ballontine. Tie the ends of the cling film and refrigerate for 6 hours to bind the fillets together.

Bring a pan of water to a boil, blanch the wrapped fish for 1 minute, and plunge into ice-cold water immediately in order to prevent any further cooking. Carefully unwrap the ballontine and cut into 1-cm-thick slices. Cover with clingfilm and place in the fridge until needed.

To Serve

10 g (⅓ oz.) reserved sand
reserved ponzu
2 g codium seaweed
2 g *hijiki* seaweed
2 g red *tosaka* seaweed
1 slice yellowtail
1 slice mackerel
2 sea jelly beans
2 samphire pieces, trimmed
1 oyster leaf, halved
2 monk's beard leaves
2 ice lettuce leaves
abalone

Place the sand on a plate and use a rigid card or spatula to shape it into a vertical strip about 1 in. (2 cm) wide. Toss the codium, hijiki, and red tosaka seaweeds in the ponzu separately, and drain on kitchen paper. Place the codium, hijiki and red tosaka seaweeds in piles at the top edge, middle and bottom edge of the sand. Place the yellow tail and the mackerel on top of the seaweed, leaving one pile for the abalone.

To cook abalone, heat a grill pan until very hot. Lightly coat the abalone in grapeseed oil, then sear the abalone, flat side first, then the other side, 30 seconds per side. Allow to cool slightly, slice, and place 3 slices over the remaining pile of seaweed.

Garnish the dish by placing the jelly beans, samphire, oyster leaf, monk's beard and ice lettuce on the sand, in between the piles of seaweed. Drizzle a little ponzu on top of the pieces of mackerel, yellow tail and abalone.

SCALLOP *Birch Syrup, Bergamot and Coral Royale*

A caramelized scallop is served alongside what looks exactly like its twin but is in fact a ring of daikon radish braised in scallop stock and filled with a bergamot-scented scallop emulsion. Finished with verjus and kombu and garnished with kombu, glazed sesame seeds, onion gel and scallop strands that have been "hammed" by brining and drying, then firming them in a sous-vide machine, this is a dish with a delicate but intense umami flavor.

For the Onion Gel

5 finely sliced large Spanish onions
Gellan F

Preheat a water bath to 185°F (85°C).

Place the sliced onions into a vacuum bag and seal under full pressure. Cook in the water bath for 96 hours.

Remove the contents from the bag, place on a piece of muslin and allow to strain suspended over a bowl. This takes about an hour. Weigh the liquid and set aside 1% of this amount of Gellan F.

Place the onion liquid into a Thermomix and set the temperature at 195°F (90°C). Add the calculated amount of Gellan F and blitz for 2 minutes on a medium setting. Allow to cool over an ice water bath. Once set, return the mixture to a clean. Thermomix and blitz to a smooth gel. Pass this mixture through a fine sieve and set aside until needed.

For the Caramelized Scallop Stock

20 scallops
2 g salt
5 g bonito flakes
grapeseed oil

Place the scallops in a strainer and rinse well under cold running water until the draining liquid runs clear.

Add the salt to the scallops and mix well. Allow them to stand for 5 minutes, before rinsing well one last time. Drain the the scallops and pat dry.

Place scallops into a pan, cover with a lid and allow them to gently cook until they start to release their moisture. Remove the scallops and strain off and discard this liquid. Heat a small amount of oil in the same pan and return the scallops, caramelizing them well without drying them out.

At this point, add 500 g water to the pan and bring to a boil. Simmer for 3 minutes and then remove from the heat. Add the bonito flakes and allow the mixture to steep for 20 minutes. Pass the mixture through a chinois, forcing the liquid through with a pestle.

Allow to cool until needed.

For the Daikon Braising Liquid

70 g mirin
160 g reserved caramelized scallop stock

Flame the mirin and allow to cool. Combine with the scallop stock and set aside until needed.

For the Daikon

3 to 4 large daikon radishes
Reserved daikon braising liquid

Preheat a water bath to 185°F (85°C).

Peel the daikon and cut into 1½ in. (4 cm) thick portions. Place each portion into a vacuum bag, along with 20 g of the daikon braising liquid in each bag. Seal under full pressure. Cook in the water bath for 1 hour 30 minutes. Allow to cool and remove from the bag. Punch each portion with a 1½ in. (4 cm) diameter ring, and then punch those discs with a 1 in. (2 cm) diameter ring in the center. Place these hollow daikon rings in a sealed container lined with paper towels and reserve until needed.

For the Coral Royale Emulsion

200 g (7 oz.) scallop roe
4 g salt
5 g bergamot zest
108 g grapeseed oil
8 g sesame seed oil

Blitz the scallop roe with 90 g of water, salt and bergamot zest until smooth. Combine the grapeseed and sesame seed oil and slowly and gradually add

them to the mixture until fully emulsified. Pass the mixture through a fine chinoise and reserve until needed.

For the "fake scallop"

Reserved cooked daikon rings
Reserved coral royale emulsion

Place the daikon rings on a tray and slide 1½ in. (4 cm) acetate discs underneath each one to ensure there is no leaking. Fill the daikon to the top with the roe emulsion and cover with a second acetate disc on top of each opening.

Cook in a steamer until the royale has set. This takes approximately 15 minutes. Reserve these "fake scallops."

For the kombu / flour mix

30 g (1 oz.) finely ground salt kombu
20 g (⅔ oz.) powdered, *tamari*-glazed sesame seeds
40 g (1⅓ oz.) plain flour
10 g (⅓ oz.) kombu powder

To make the finely ground salt kombu, place salt kombu in a container with liquid nitrogen. Strain the nitro off and transfer the mixture to a Thermomix. Blend on high speed for 17 minutes. Place the mixture on a dehydrator tray and allow to dry overnight. Repeat this process with the glazed sesame seeds.

Combine the powdered salt kombu and the tamari-glazed sesame seeds with the flour and the kombu powder.

Set aside to use when finishing the "fake scallops."

For the Sesame Seed and Kombu Mixture

15 g (½ oz.) glazed sesame seeds
50 g (1⅔ oz.) chopped salt kombu

Combine the glazed sesame seeds and the chopped salt kombu. Set aside until needed.

For the Tamari-glazed Sesame Seeds

375 g *iri goma* (Japanese roasted white sesame seeds)
50 g (1⅔ oz.) isomalt
tamari soy sauce
11 g icing sugar

Pre-warm the panning machine on half-heat setting.

Place the sesame seeds into a China Cap and sift out any powder or broken seeds.

Combine the isomalt with 20 g water in a small saucepan and heat to dissolve the isomalt completely. Once it has reached 70° brix, add tamari sauce gradually, until the mixture reads 63° brix. Set aside.

Place the sesame seeds and the icing sugar into the panning machine and run on medium speed with a three-quarters warm air-flow.

Add one 15 ml pipette of syrup to the seeds in the panning machine and allow to fully incorporate before adding the next pipette. In between additions, use a rubber spatula or wooden spoon to continuously separate the mixture and prevent clumping. Continue this process until all the seeds are glazed and separated. There should be no clusters. This process can take up to 2 hours. Remove and store in a sealed container until needed.

For the Black Sesame, Birch and Verjus Mixture

30 g (1 oz.) black sesame tahini
100 g reduced verjus (thick syrup stage having reached 250°F/120°C)
100 g birch syrup

To make the tahini, grind the black sesame seeds to a smooth paste.

Dilute the reduced verjus with birch syrup and add the tahini. Set aside until needed.

For the Bergamot Salt

100 g (3½ oz.) sea salt
3 g bergamot zest

Combine the sea salt and the bergamot zest and store in a sealed container until needed.

For the Scallop Ham

300 g (10 oz.) salt
100 g (3½ oz.) white caster sugar
120 g water × 2
2 whole scallops

Combine the salt and sugar with 120 g water to make a brine. Place the scallops in the brine for 1 hour 30 minutes. Rinse well.

Place the brined and rinsed scallops into a dehydrator set at 150°F (65°C) for 48 hours.

Remove the dried scallops and seal them in a vacuum bag with another 120 g water for 7 hours. Remove them from the bag, pat dry and seal again in a vacuum bag, this time refrigerating overnight.

Remove the scallops from the bag and pull apart into fine, single-fiber strands. Reserve half of these strands for serving, and place the other half back into the dehydrator until crunchy and dry. Reserve for serving

To serve

Olive oil
1 Scallop
75 g verjus
Freshly squeezed bergamot juice
Reserved bergamot salt
Reserved cooked "fake scallop"
Reserved kombu/flour mix
Egg white wash
Ground *panko* bread crumbs
Reserved onion gel
Reserved sesame and kombu mixture
Reserved scallop ham fibers
Reserved dried scallop ham fibers
Reserved black sesame, birch and verjus mixture

Heat a small amount of oil in a pan and fry the scallop presentation side-down until nicely colored, before turning (only once). Once the internal temperature of the scallop reaches 115°F (46°C), remove the scallop and set aside, allowing the residual heat to bring the core temperature to 122°F (50°C).

Drain the oil from the pan and add the verjus, reducing until to a syrup. Strain the reduced verjus into a separate container and finish with several drop of bergamot juice, to taste.

To plate, brush the non-presentation side of the scallop with the verjus/bergamot glaze and season the presentation side with bergamot salt.

In the meantime, cover the top of the "fake scallop" with the kombu/flour mixture. Brush with the egg white wash and top with the panko bread crumbs. Shallow fry these "scallops" crumb-side down until golden brown. Drain and set aside.

Pipe a thin layer of onion gel onto one side of the plate and sprinkle the sesame and kombu mixture onto it. Top with a combination of dried and non-dried scallop ham fibers.

Place the cooked, dressed scallop next to the onion gel and the "fake scallop" alongside it.

Pipe a large dot of the black sesame, birch and verjus mixture next to the two plated "scallops."

POT-AU-FEU

Marmite is a familiar umami food in Western Europe and Australasia. Here dashi made from generous quantities of vegetables is combined with Marmite stock to produce a memorable *pot-au-feu*.

For the Marmite Consommé

- 1.5 kg (3 lbs.) strained brown butter
- 2 kg (4½ lbs.) finely sliced sweet onions
- 2 kg (4½ lbs.) finely sliced leeks (white parts only)
- 1 kg (2¼ lbs.) finely sliced carrots
- 1.5 kg (3 lbs.) full-bodied red wine
- 100 g egg whites
- 9 g salt
- 20 g sherry vinegar
- 10 g Marmite
- 1 g finely ground and sifted black pepper

Gently heat 1 lb. (500 g) of the brown butter in a pressure cooker and sweat the onions, leeks and carrots until softened.

In the meantime, in a separate saucepan, bring the wine to a boil and flame off the alcohol. Allow to reduce to 500 g and then add it to the softened vegetables, along with 500 g of water. Secure the lid of the pressure cooker and cook under full pressure for 2 hours.

Remove from the heat and allow the pressure cooker to depressurise before opening the lid and straining the contents through a fine sieve, discarding the vegetables. Use a hand blender to blitz in the remaining 1 kg (2¼ lbs.) of brown butter. Store the stock in the fridge overnight.

Remove the fat that has risen to the top of the chilled stock and discard.

In a clean bowl, whisk the egg whites to soft-peak stage and then add to the broth, whisking until well incorporated.

Place the stock into a saucepan and bring to a gentle simmer, allowing the egg white foam to float to the top and form a raft. After 20 minutes, slowly ladle the consommé through a coffee filter. Return the clear consommé to a gentle simmer and repeat the process until no residual egg white coagulates.

Set aside 210 g of this unseasoned consommé for use in the horseradish royale.

Weigh out 1 kg of the remaining consommé. Add 9 g salt, 20 g sherry vinegar, 10 g Marmite and 1 g of the sifted black pepper. Combine well and pass this seasoned consommé through a fine mesh filter bag. Set aside until needed.

For the Horseradish Royale

- 210 g reserved unseasoned Marmite consommé
- 200 g whole milk
- 110 g egg yolk
- 28 g egg white
- 7 g salt
- 1.5 g freshly ground and sifted black pepper
- 65 g creamed horseradish

Place all the ingredients in a bowl and blitz using a hand blender. Pass the mixture through a fine sieve and refrigerate until needed.

For the "Marrowbone"

- 6 to 8 Daikon radishes

Choose sections of the daikon that are large enough to carve out cylinders measuring 2 in. (4 to 5 cm) in diameter and at least 3 in. (8 cm) tall. Using a ring cutter and a paring knife, cut out the cylinder and using the back edge of a knife, scrape the sides of the cylinder to form a smooth, bone-like shape.

Use a Parisian scoop to begin hollowing out the cylinder, then use a small knife to scrape the rest of the inside so that the edges of the "bone" are a uniform thickness of 0.5 mm. Ensure that it has not been hollowed all the way through to the bottom, to avoid the custard filling leaking out during cooking.

Cook them in a steamer until tender. Set aside until ready to complete the "marrowbone."

For the Vegetables

Variety of seasonal vegetables

Scrape or peel the vegetables as necessary. You may wish to halve some of the vegetables, depending on their size. Set these vegetables aside in the fridge until ready to cook.

For the Gribiche

15 g (½ oz.) brunoise-cut gherkins
15 g (½ oz.) minced capers
15 g (½ oz.) brunoise-cut shallots
4 g finely sliced tarragon leaves
8 g finely chopped parsley
8 g finely sliced chives
244 g whole milk
34 g National Starch Flogel 60
28 g dijon mustard
15 g lemon juice
15 chardonnay vinegar
10 g salt
0.5 g freshly ground and sifted black pepper
276 g grapeseed oil
1 hard-boiled egg (brunoise-cut white; yolk passed through a tamis)
100 g plain flour
1 egg white
100 g *panko* bread crumbs

Mix the gherkins, capers, shallots and herbs and set aside.

Place the milk into a saucepan and add the Flogel 60. Use a hand blender to blitz well. Heat the mixture to 212°F (100°C), stirring occasionally. Once the mixture starts boiling, allow to boil for 30 seconds, stirring continuously. Remove from the heat and using the hand blender, add the mustard, lemon juice, vinegar, 8 g of the salt and the pepper, blitzing well. Slowly incorporate the oil with the hand blender and continue to blitz until the mixture cools.

Once the mixture has cooled and thickened, fold in the reserved herb mixture, along with the bruncise-cut egg white and passed yolk. Transfer the mixture to a shallow container and cover. Allow to gel in the fridge for several hours.

Remove the gelled gribiche and cut into ½ in. (1.5 cm) cubes.

Sift the flour and the remaining 2 g of salt into a bowl. In a separate bowl, lightly whip the egg white with a little water. In a third bowl, gently rub the panko bread crumbs to create finer crumbs.

Lightly coat the gribiche cubes in the seasoned flour. Dip into the egg white mixture and finally coat evenly with the crushed breadcrumbs, lightly patting the crumbs into the cube.

Place the cubes in the fridge in an airtight container for several hours to firm up.

For the Crispy Chervil

Grapeseed oil
40 Chervil leaves

Wrap a dinner plate tightly with cling film and brush with the oil. Place individually picked chervil leaves on the cling film in a single layer, without touching. Cook in the microwave on a medium power for 4 minutes, and then increase the power for an additional 5 minutes.

To serve

Reserved hollow daikon "bones"
Reserved horseradish royale mixture
Reserved Marmite consommé
Reserved seasonal vegetables
Unsalted butter
Girolles
Grapeseed oil
Reserved gribiche cubes
Extra virgin olive oil
5 lemon thyme leaves
Reserved crispy chervil
Salt and freshly ground black pepper

Place the daikon "bones" onto a tray and fill with the horseradish royale mixture. Cover with cling film and place into a steamer on medium heat for 15 minutes.

In the meantime, place the seasonal vegetables into a steamer until cooked through. Remove and season with salt and black pepper.

Heat a pan filled three-quarters of the way with grapeseed oil to 350°F (180°C) and fry the cubes of gribiche until golden. Drain on paper towels and season with salt.

To cook the girolles, lightly fry them in a small amount of butter. Drain on paper towels and season with salt.

Reheat the Marmite consommé and keep warm.

When the daikon "bones" are cooked, trim the top to an even layer and place in the centre of a warm, shallow bowl. Depending on the size of the daikon "bones," two per portion in the centre will also work well. Arrange the vegetables around the "bone."

Pour a small amount of warm consommé into the bowl, covering the bottom of the bowl. Drizzle with a good-quality olive oil and garnish with lemon thyme leaves.

Serve with the gribiche alongside in a paper-lined cornet that has been placed in a receptacle that will hold it upright. Garnish with the crispy chervil leaves.

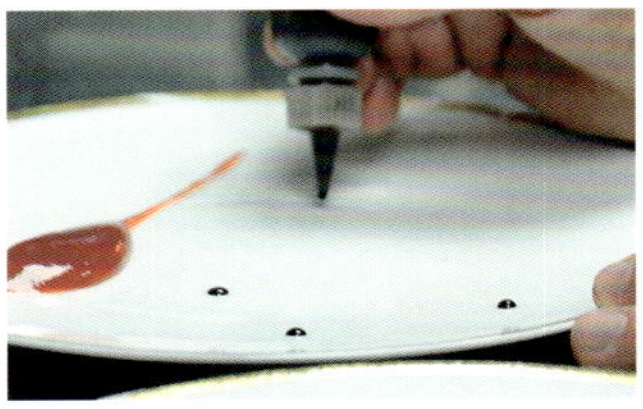

ROAST FOIE GRAS *Gooseberry, Confit Kombu and Crab Biscuit*

Foie gras prepared in a water bath is fully cooked yet deliciously moist. When served on a kombu confit and topped with crispy crab biscuit tuiles and gooseberry sauce, the result is exquisite umami harmony.

For the Crab reduction

4 kg (9 lbs.) live etrile crabs
⅓ cup plus 4 tsp. (100 ml) olive oil

Plunge the crabs in cold tap water for 10 minutes. In the meantime, heat the olive oil over medium-high heat in a pressure cooker and fry the crabs until nutty and toasty and all the crab juices have evaporated.

Add 6.6 liters of water and bring to a boil, skimming off all scum and impurities that rise to the surface. Secure the lid and cook under full pressure for 1 hour.

Remove from the heat allow the pressure cooker to depressurise before opening the lid. Allow the stock to stand for 10 minutes before straining.

Place in the blast chiller, and once completely chilled, remove all fat that accumulates on the surface. Return the stock to a saucepan and reduce over medium heat, and switching pans when the stock becomes cloudy and impurities are left on the sides.

Reduce to a treacle-like consistency and allow to cool. Set the crab reduction aside for use in the crab biscuit tuille, as well as the crab and balsamic reduction.

For the Crab Biscuit Tuille

To make the baked crab biscuit
100 g (3½ oz.) brown butter
100 g egg whites
100 g (3½ oz.) plain flour
100 g reserved crab reduction
480 g maple syrup

Using a hand blender, blitz the brown butter and egg whites. Add sifted flour and mix until smooth. Using a spatula, mix in the crab reduction, combining well. Stir in the syrup. Cover and refrigerate for at least 6 hours.

Preheat the oven to 300°F (150°C). Spread the batter thinly, using the back of a flat spoon, over the surface of a silicone mat, which has been placed onto a tray. Bake until golden brown, then transfer the biscuits to a dry surface. Store in an airtight container with packets of silica gel.

To make the sugar base
250 g isomalt
250 g glucose syrup 42DE

Combine the isomalt and glucose in a small pan and heat to 315°F (158°C).

Pour this hot caramel on to a silicone mat and allow to cool completely. Once cooled, break the hardened caramel into smaller pieces and keep in an airtight container until needed.

To finish the crab biscuit tuille
400 g reserved sugar base pieces
80 g reserved baked crab biscuits

Place the sugar base pieces into a Thermomix and blitz to a fine powder. Add the baked crab biscuits and use the pulse setting to blitz the biscuits into small crumbs—not to a fine powder.

Preheat the oven to 300°F (150°C). Transfer the powder to a fine sieve to dust the surface of a silicone mat with an even layer about 1 mm thick. Place in the oven until the powder melts.

Remove the caramel from the oven and set aside to cool. Once cold, break into shards about 3 in. × 1½ in. (8 cm × 4 cm). Place these tuilles in an airtight container with silica gel.

For the Crab and Balsamic Reduction

1 kg balsamic vinegar
500 g reserved crab reduction

Place the balsamic vinegar into the bowl of a Rocket evaporator and reduce by half. Remove the vinegar from the

Rocket and mix in an equal amount of the reserved crab reduction. Store in a small squeeze sauce bottle.

For the Gooseberry Purée

To make the gooseberry juice
7.5 kg (16.5 lbs.) gooseberries
900 g fructose

Gently squash the gooseberries with your hands and combine with the fructose. Allow to macerate for an hour.

Transfer the gooseberries to a pot and heat to 160°F (70°C), stirring regularly. Hold at this temperature for 30 minutes, tasting regularly for the desired level of tartness. (You may need to do this in two batches.)

Remove from the heat and pass through a fine sieve, pressing lightly to allow all juice to be extracted. Cool the juice and divide into a 1.5 kg batch for use in the fluid gel, and a 3 kg batch for use in the Rocket.

To make the gooseberry fluid gel
1.5 kg reserved gooseberry juice
15 g Gellan F

Pour 750 g of the gooseberry juice into the Thermomix set at 195°F (90°C). Add 7.5 g Gellan F and blitz for 2 minutes on a medium setting. Allow to cool over an iced water bath. Once set, return the mixture to a clean Thermomix and blitz to a smooth gel. Pass this mixture through a fine sieve and reserve for use in the purée.

Repeat the process once more with the remaining juice and Gellan F.

To reduce the gooseberry juice
3 kg reserved gooseberry juice

Place the gooseberry juice into the bowl of the Rocket and reduce to 2 kg.

To finish the gooseberry purée
1.5 kg reserved gooseberry fluid gel
2 kg reserved (Rocket-reduced) gooseberry juice

Using a hand blender, blitz the gooseberry fluid gel with the reduced gooseberry juice. Cover and place the finished purée in the fridge until needed.

For the Confit Ma-Kombu

10 sheets dehydrated *ma-kombu*
250 g sake
200 g mirin
750 g dashi
500 g soy sauce
50 g golden caster sugar
350 g glucose syrup

Preheat the oven to 250°F (120°C). Soak the kombu in water for approximately 20 minutes.

Remove from the water and slice each kombu sheet into 4 squares. Set aside. In the meantime, combine the sake and mirin in a pot and flame off the alcohol.

In a pot, combine the flamed sake and mirin, dashi, soy sauce, golden caster sugar and glucose. Bring to a boil.

Add the kombu and bring back to a boil, before removing from the stove top and covering with a muslin and cartouche. Place in the oven for 6 hours.

Check the kombu—it should still have a slight bite. Once the kombu has cooked, check the braising liquid for consistency. If necessary, remove the kombu from the liquid and reduce the liquid to a light syrup consistency. If it has reduced too far, add a little water.

Keep the kombu in the liquid. Square off the kombu neatly and reserve all trimmings. Finely dice these trimmings for use in the garnish.

For the Tamari-glazed Sesame Seeds

(see p. 28)

For the Foie Gras

5 × 80 g cryogenically-frozen portions of foie gras, sealed individually in vacuum bags

Preheat a water bath to 150°F (65°C) and a second water bath to 140°F (60°C).

Place the frozen foie gras into the water bath and allow to reach an internal temperature of 150°F (65°C). Transfer to the water bath set at 140°F (60°C) and hold there for no longer than 30 minutes before serving.

To Serve

- Reserved braised *ma-kombu* trimmings, finely diced
- Reserved *tamari*-glazed sesame seeds
- Chives, finely sliced
- Salt kombu, finely chopped
- Cooked foie gras, 40 g per portion
- Reserved confit *ma-kombu* squares
- Reserved crab biscuit tuilles
- Reserved gooseberry purée
- Reserved crab and balsamic reduction
- Salt
- Freshly ground white pepper
- Freshly ground black pepper
- Freshly ground long pepper
- Sheep sorrel

Combine equal amounts of finely diced ma-kombu trimmings, glazed sesame seeds and chives. Add a smaller amount of finely diced salt kombu than that of the ma-kombu and set this sesame mix aside.

Remove the foie gras from the bags and pat dry. Use a blowtorch on each piece and brown as quickly and evenly as possible. Slice each portion into two even pieces, so you are left with 10 portions of foie gras, 40 g each. Slice each 40 g portion into 3 even pieces. Season with salt and freshly ground white pepper.

Place a square of braised ma-kombu on each plate, and place the sliced foie gras on top of the kombu. Top the foie gras with the sesame mix and carefully place 2 crab biscuit tuilles in between the slices. Season with sea salt, freshly ground black pepper and freshly ground long pepper.

Drag a spoonful of gooseberry purée across the plate alongside the foie gras, and drop several crab and balsamic reduction dots around the plate.

Garnish with sheep sorrel and serve immediately.

SaQuaNa Honfleur

ALEXANDRE BOURDAS

It would not be truthful for me to declare that I am always thinking of umami whenever I am creating a new dish. However, I am aware of the foods that contain umami, and I do like it very much. Even when I am not thinking specifically about umami, I use many umami-rich ingredients in my cooking. I also take advantage of the synergies between umami and other tastes.

My first conscious experience of umami was when I sampled some powdered dashi with a Japanese friend, who told me about the name of this taste. My immediate reaction was, "This is amazing! I want more!" It was not the first time that I had tried Japanese dashi, but it seemed much better than anything I remembered. Consequently the impact of that experience became the basis of my thinking about umami.

If I were to define umami, I would call it a comfortable taste, a taste that brings pleasure to the palate. Moreover, it is a taste that can be enjoyed just by itself. So I use it with the aim not of balancing other flavors, but of giving diners greater pleasure from their food. In my own words, I would describe umami as a fusion of taste and aroma that spreads from the back of the tongue to the nose, creating a mellow sensation that leaves the eater wanting more. A chef who is familiar with umami and its sources can use it rationally and skillfully, selecting ingredients to bring it out more strongly—or, as appropriate, to keep it from becoming overpowering. Just as with sourness and sweetness, umami ceases to be delicious when it is too strong. To use it effectively, we must be aware of the level of umami in each ingredient and adjust the amounts accordingly.

There is more to my cooking than just umami, of course. I have been using it for some years now along with new techniques based on my experience, providing a full range of my feelings and creative sense. I want to keep making dishes that tap the power of umami in original ways, ranging freely beyond the bounds of convention and genre.

RYE BRIOCHE WITH SEAWEED, GRILLED SARDINES, SOY SAUCE, SPINACH, AND ROQUEFORT CHEESE

Sardines are brushed with soy sauce, grilled, and accompanied by brioche with umami-rich *nori* worked into the dough. Ocean's bounty joins mountain's blessing (Roquefort cheese) for a superbly intense taste.

SERVES 8

Rye Brioche with Seaweed

Makes about 60 portions
200 g (7 oz.) unsalted butter
10 g (⅓ oz.) fresh yeast
10 g (⅓ oz.) granulated sugar
10 g (⅓ oz.) salt
70 g milk
About 2 tsp. chopped dried seaweed such as *nori*, *dulse*, or *aosa*
500 g (17½ oz.) T55 flour or all-purpose flour
50 g (1⅔ oz.) rye flour
6 eggs
4 tsp. olive oil

8 sardines
Soy sauce
100 g (3½ oz.) spinach
100 g (3½ oz.) farm-fresh yogurt

Crumbled Roquefort cheese, lemon zest, baby watercress, and pickled *sansho* peppercorns for topping

Start making brioche 12 hours before baking. Soften the butter at room temperature. Tear the yeast into small pieces and dissolve in 1 Tbsp. of warm water. Dissolve the sugar and salt into the milk. Add the chopped seaweed to the mixture of T55 flour and rye flour, and combine with all the other ingredients. Knead, let the dough rise, punch down, and make rolls, each 18 g. Allow to proof in molds about 1½ to 1¾ in. (3.5 to 4 cm) in diameter.

Meanwhile, remove scales, head, and guts from the sardines, rinse, and cut into fillets. Lightly sprinkle with salt and keep in a refrigerator.

Bake the proofed brioche at 280°F (140°C) for 15 minutes.

Cut the stem and veins off the spinach and sauté in butter. Cut the sardines into approximately same size as the diameter of the brioche, and grill or sear with a gas burner while basting with the soy sauce.

To assemble, place a brioche on each plate and top with 1 tsp. of yogurt and some of the spinach leaves. Top with the sardine pieces and garnish with the Roquefort, lemon zest, baby watercress, and pickled sansho peppercorns.

SLICED RAW VEAL WITH WHITE JUS, PESTO, AND AVEYRON SALAMI

My childhood home of Aveyron is a mountainous pastoral region. In this recipe, calves raised there are made into carpaccio and served with aged salami. The beef jus with its concentrated umami and the equally umami-rich salami make a powerful combination.

SERVES 8

White Jus

350 g (11⅔ oz.) scraps or trimmings of veal round
90 g (3 oz.) butter
30 g (1 oz.) garlic, minced
90 g (3 oz.) onion, minced
1 Tbsp. white roux
300 g white veal stock
100 g fresh cream

Pesto

20 g (⅔ oz.) almond flour
100 g (3½ oz.) Parmigiano Reggiano cheese
3 g garlic
5 g parsley
8 g basil leaves
50 g olive oil
Salt and pepper

300 g (10½ oz.) veal round, preferably Aveyron, semi-frozen for easier slicing
Aveyron salami
Basil leaves

To make the white jus, sauté the veal scraps in butter, without allowing them to brown, and then stir in the garlic and onion. Add the white veal stock, fresh cream, and white roux. Cook in a 340°F (170°C) oven for an hour and strain.

To make the pesto, mix all the ingredients in a food processor.

To assemble, thinly slice the veal round using a meat slicer and lightly sprinkle with salt. Slice the salami. Place a ring mold, about 4 in. (10 cm) in diameter, on a serving dish, spread the veal slices around in the mold to make a large circle, and remove the mold. Repeat for each serving. Arrange the salami slices, pesto, and basil leaves on the veal. Sprinkle with salt and olive oil and pour the cooled white jus over top.

HERB "RAVIOLI" WITH IBERICO PORK RAGOÛT, IBERICO HAM, FRESH CHEESE WITH ARUGULA, AND AGED GOAT CHEESE

Goat's cheese acquires more intense umami with aging. Combining different umami components—inosinate in pork, glutamate in cured ham—creates overall synergy.

SERVES 8

Pasta Dough

Makes 15 to 20 rounds

175 g (6¼ oz.) all purpose flour
4 g salt
10 g (⅓ oz.) unsalted butter
1 egg
35 g milk
15 g olive oil
5 g parsley, minced
2 g coriander, minced
2 g celery leaves, minced
2 g tarragon, minced

Iberico Pork Ragoût

200 g (7 oz.) Iberico pork loin
Salt and pepper
30 g (1 oz.) unsalted butter
1 clove garlic, minced
4 tsp. pork jus

Arugula Cheese Mixture

40 g (1⅓ oz.) *faisselle* fresh cheese
50 g (1⅔ oz.) arugula, minced
15 g olive oil

2 slices hamon Iberico
Aged goat cheese, minced Italian parsley, and pepper for garnish

To make the "ravioli," first mix all the ingredients of the pasta dough except the minced herbs, then mix in the herbs at the end. Roll out into thin sheets using a pasta machine and cut into 8 circles with a 4 in. (10 cm) ring mold.

To make Iberico pork ragoût, lightly sprinkle the pork with salt and pepper, add butter, and grind using a meat grinder. Sauté the ground pork with a little butter and stir in the garlic and pork jus.

To make the fresh cheese mixture, mix all the ingredients, season with salt to taste, and spoon into a pastry bag.

Cook the pasta circles in boiled salted water for several seconds and drain.

To assemble, pipe out the faisselle mixture onto each dish. Divide the Iberico ham, Iberico pork ragoût, and Italian parsley into 8 servings and plate alternately. Cover each with a pasta circle. Sprinkle with ground goat cheese, minced Italian parsley, and pepper.

COCONUT CHICKEN BROTH WITH POACHED LOBSTER, LOVAGE, CORIANDER, AND KAFFIR LIME OIL

This lobster was caught by me that morning. Growing in nutrient-rich waters, Normandy lobsters are acknowledged to be some of the world's finest. This soup featuring coconut and herb flavors is also a popular choice at my restaurant.

SERVES 8

Coconut Chicken Broth

1 L chicken broth
40 g (1⅓ oz.) fresh coconut powder
1 stalk lemongrass
1 Homard lobster, 500 to 600 g (19 oz.)

200 g (7 oz.) spinach
Lovage, leaves only
Coriander, leaves only
Kaffir lime oil
Lime juice
Lime zest
Powdered Espelette chili (piment d'Espelette)
Fleur de sel

Bring the chicken broth to a boil, add the fresh coconut powder and lemongrass, and stop the heat. Cover, leave for 30 minutes to steep, and strain.

Cook the lobster in boiled salted water for 3 minutes. Shock in ice water to cool and drain. Remove the shell and cut into rounds. Keep at room temperature.

Pick only leaves of the spinach and sauté with butter. Cut the lovage into fine strips.

To assemble, place the lovage, spinach, and coriander in each bowl and drizzle with kaffir lime oil and lime juice. Place the lobster piece on top. Sprinkle with lime zest, powdered Espelette chili, and fleur de sel. Finish with the coconut chicken broth.

Traditional sources of umami in Nordic cuisine

Canned umami: the Danes' preferred "umami bomb"

Denmark may hold the world record in consumption of canned umami: the 5 million Danes eat 70 million cans of mackerel in tomato sauce every year! Mackerel in tomato sauce is a perfect "umami bomb" with plenty of synergy: glutamate from the tomato sauce and inosinate from the cooked mackerel. Traditionally it is eaten on rye bread, but modern chefs have also reinterpreted the tradition and brought it into fine dining.

A modern interpretation of "canned mackerel in tomato sauce": fried mackerel, morels, sun-ripened tomato, burned potato, and white asparagus, topped with fermented mackerel fish sauce, a veritable "umami bomb."

Traditional Nordic umami: an ancient need for preservation

The Nordic countries have a living tradition of consuming strange (and smelly) food that is fermented, dried, and aged as a consequence of the pre-refrigeration need for preserving perishable foodstuffs. Despite the smell, the delicious umami easily compensates for the odor. The best-known examples are the Swedish *surströmming*, a fermented Baltic herring conserved in cans that often bulge and are at the brink of explosion; Norwegian *rakfisk*, salted and fermented trout, whitefish, char, or perch; Icelandic *hákarl*, fermented shark; Faroe Island's *skerpikjøt*, dried and fermented mutton; as well as Danish *modnet sild*, whole herring salted and fermented by the enzymes from its own entrails. Modern Nordic *gravlax* or *gravad laks* is lightly marinated fresh salmon, but its name reflects that the fish was originally fermented by burying it in a dirt pit. In this way, *gravlax* shares a historical development similar to sushi, which originated as a way of preserving fish by fermenting it in cooked rice.

Ole G. Mouritsen
Professor Ph.D. DSc, University of Southern Denmark and Nordic Food Lab

Klavs Styrbæk
Chef, *Styrbæks*, Denmark

Umami from an agricultural nation

Denmark was until recently a predominantly agricultural country, and it still produces large amounts of fresh and processed foodstuffs for export. Many of these products are appreciated for their unique qualities, not least their taste. The most well-known are probably Danish bacon (rich in inosinate) and Danish cheeses (rich in glutamate).

Most traditional Danish cheeses are semi-soft or hard cheeses that are matured from a few months up to several years. Danish Blue (*Danablu*) is a highly valued, soft blue cheese with large amounts of glutamate. It is often used in the traditional kitchen to adjust the umami of brown gravy based on a stock made from meat, bones, and vegetables. The traditional Danish dairy industry is currently experiencing a revival, led by a vanguard of small dairies that experiment with new cheese products based on organic and in some cases biodynamic milk. Some producers using raw milk have now challenged the long tradition of using only pasteurized milk. Gouda-type cheeses like *Lagret Høost* and *Vesterhavsost* deserve special mention, as well as the new gastronomic series of raw milk cheeses, *Arla Unika*.

An umami-rich simple lunch: aged hard cheese, sourdough rye bread, and wheat beer.

Cheese in Denmark is traditionally eaten with open sandwiches made from dark rye bread. This bread itself is rich in umami. Fermented from a sourdough starter that often is kept alive for years, rye bread complements a simple lunch meal with aged cheese and wheat beer.

LITERATURE

O.G. Mouritsen & K. Styrbæk, *Umami. Uncovering the Secrets of the Fifth Taste*, (New York: Columbia University Press, 2014).

NOR AME

MICHAEL ANTHONY

Gramercy Tavern New York

TH

RICA

DAVID KINCH

Manresa Los Gatos

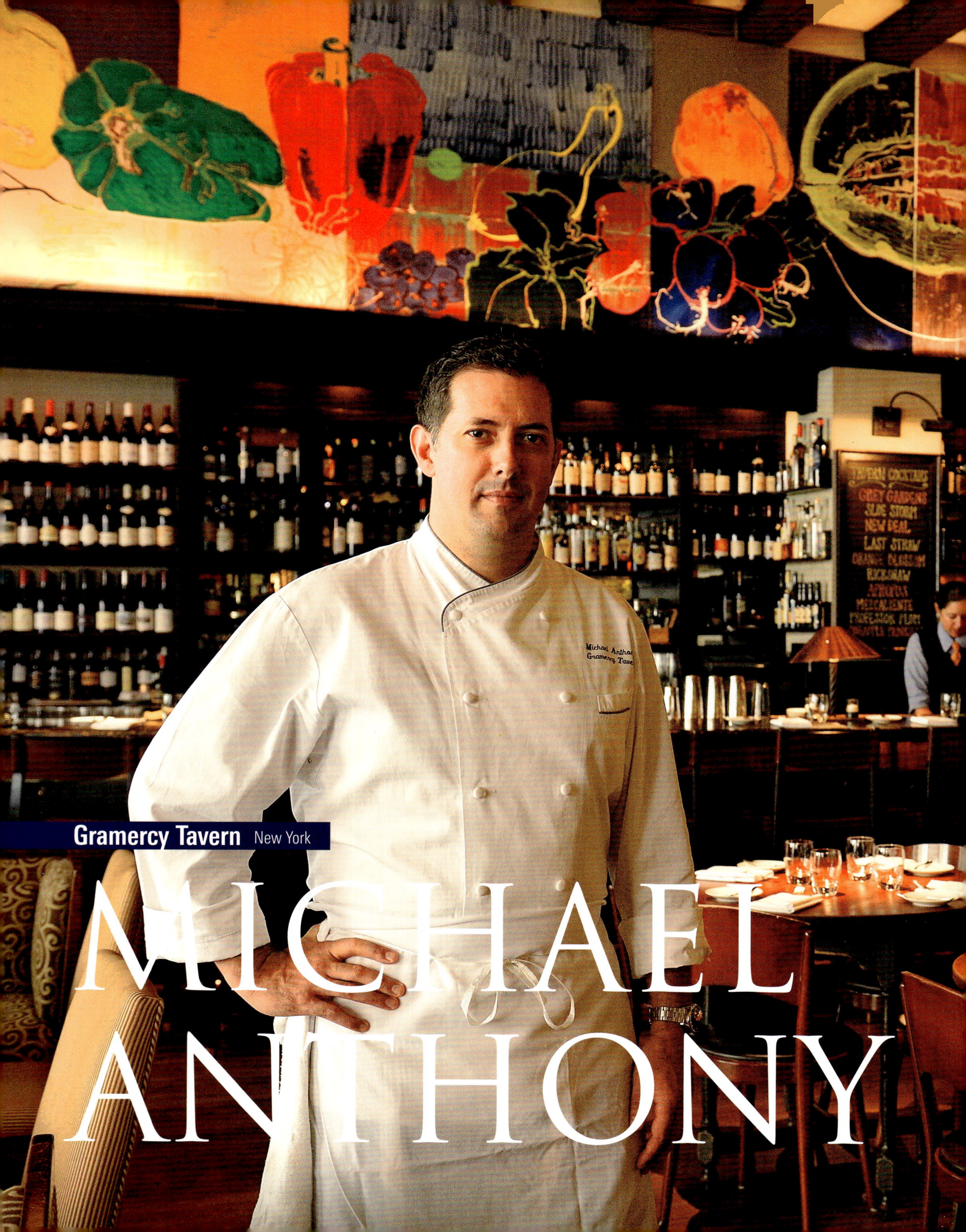

Gramercy Tavern New York

MICHAEL ANTHONY

To express umami to a person who doesn't know the taste, I usually use the word "earthy." It's not a great descriptor, because "earthy" really means musty and mushroom-like, but it's one way I find myself describing umami. I never use the word "meaty," because when I think about umami, it's much more soft. It's very difficult to describe. In fact, we actually use the word "umami" to describe the taste of umami, so we use it as an adjective as well as a noun. It's a natural deliciousness to a dish that mostly comes from glutamate.

I am always trying to find a way to cook a distinctive American style at Gramercy Tavern, even when there is an undercurrent of Japanese spirit. We use some important ingredients like dashi and kombu, but I don't ever want to cross that line of making the food here fusion, because it's not! Still, it's okay to be inspired by a number of aspects that are typically Japanese. The ultimate question is: how do we tell a seasonal American story? So we've taken some ideas from Japan, but we've made them our own.

A good example is *nukazuke* (vegetables pickled by burying them in salted rice bran), which requires much more attention than most pickling techniques. It's a long process, and it's difficult to control fermentation. It's like this elusive, ever-changing thing—sometimes it goes fast, sometimes it goes slow and requires our daily observation, and then sometimes it just goes bad. We serve nukazuke with scallops, and we also serve it with duck liver. We use some vinegar pickles and some salt-fermented pickles along with the nukazuke. Using pickles lets our cooking be more refreshing. We also make our own sauerkraut (which is ultimately a European recipe, but it's fermented cabbage, so it's very similar to Japanese pickling), and we serve that with buckwheat *spätzle* and a beef *kielbasa*.

Another way we borrow from Japanese cuisine: we make a mushroom purée that we finish by blending some marinated kombu into the purée. It has an indescribable, slightly smooth mouth feel from the umami, which makes it simple but delicious! Umami has given us a kind of courage to cook food with a more simple approach. It's a flavor that doesn't jump out as being sweet or sour or acidic or bitter. Umami is a way to make dishes compelling and keep them restrained. I think every cook, just as every artist, is looking to restrain or refine their crafts. It's a natural process. Discovering umami gives us a chance, like with our halibut dish, to use few ingredients, but still, when the guests eat it, there's something about it that is irresistible.

Michael Anthony

SCALLOP, *NUKAZUKE* AND POLE BEANS

One thing I got to know while living in Japan was *tsukemono.* A fermented food, *tsukemono* are a healthy umami ingredient, and I stir rice bran (*nuka*) daily to make my own. The vegetables used in this dish were pickled for seven days, imparting a subtle tang and making them easy to eat salad-style.

SERVES 4

8 large sea scallops, halved
2 cups (350 g) pole beans, blanched and diced
1 tsp. minced shallot
12 sungold tomatoes, halved
1 cup (175 g) *nukazuke* vegetables, cut into pieces (recipe below)
½ cup (120 ml) anchovy vinaigrette
2 Tbsp. trout roe
2 Tbsp. toasted, shaved almond

In a large bowl, toss the cut scallops, blanched pole beans, minced shallot, sungold tomato and nukazuke vegetables together with a little anchovy vinaigrette. Reserve some nukazuke vegetables to garnish the dish.

Serve the dressed scallop and vegetables on individual plates and garnish with shaved almonds, trout roe and the reserved nukazuke vegetables.

Nukazuke Pickles

Yields 4 qt. (4 L) ceramic pot
4 lbs. (2 kg) rice bran
4- to 6-in. (10- to 15-cm) strips kombu
¾ cup (195 g) sea salt
2 cups plus 10 cups (450 ml + 2.25 L) water
1 cup (250 g) miso, optional
Scant 2 cups (450 ml) beer (try *Hitachino*, a rice beer)
2-in. (5-cm) piece of ginger, cut into chunks
5 or 6 pc. seasonal vegetables

Toast rice bran, being careful not to burn it.

Place kombu in a large bowl. Heat 2 cups (480 ml) water to boiling and pour over kombu to rehydrate. Dissolve salt in the remaining 10 cups (2.25 L) water to make a brine.

Mix miso with a small amount of brine to make a loose paste, breaking up any lumps.

Remove the kombu from the liquid and reserve. Mix the kombu liquid and the miso with the brine. Add the liquid to the rice bran along with the ginger and kombu pieces. Mix to ensure there are no dry areas of bran.

Put the mixture into a large bowl or container. Bury whole, washed, but not peeled, vegetables in the rice bran mixture without them touching. Cover with a plate and place a weight on the plate. Cover top of container with cheesecloth and a loose lid and place in the refrigerator.

The next day, remove the weight and check the amount of liquid above the plate. If there is none, add more brine. If there is more than an inch, remove some liquid. The mixture consistency should be like wet sand. Remove the pickled vegetables and compost or discard them. Stir the mixture and add new vegetables.

Continue to replace the vegetables in this manner every day, making sure to stir up the mixture well. After about a week and a half, start to taste the vegetables that come out of the pot. When they seem like they are pickling well, add the vegetables that are intended to be served. Leave these vegetables in the pot until they are fully pickled, but continue to stir up the mixture daily.

Approximate Pickling Times

Sunchokes: 7 to 14 days
Red globe radishes: 5 days
Kale stems: 3 to 4 days
Celery Root: 14 days
Young daikon radish: 10 days to 2 weeks
Watermelon radish: 5 days
Hakurei turnips: 2 weeks

Anchovy Vinaigrette

5 anchovies, cleaned and minced
1 Tbsp. white soy sauce
2 Tbsp. white balsamic vinegar
1 Tbsp. lemon juice
¼ tsp. fish sauce
¾ cup (170 ml) olive oil, whisked slowly
2 Tbsp. garlic oil
Salt and pepper

In a blender, combine anchovy, white soy, white balsamic, lemon juice and fish sauce.

While blending, slowly drizzle in olive oil and garlic oil until well emulsified. Season to taste with salt and pepper.

MICHAEL ANTHONY

HALIBUT WITH EGGPLANT AND TOMATO WATER

Both the slow-baked halibut and tomatoes are soft to suit the texture of this dish, while miso-flavored tomato water as an umami sauce brings it all together.

SERVES 4

4 halibut filets, each 4 oz. (115 g)
2 oz. (60 g) butter
1 oz. (30 g) white miso

6 fairytale eggplants, halved lengthwise
1 Italian eggplant, diced
2 Tbsp. white balsamic vinegar
1 tsp. white miso
1 tsp. mirin
1 cup (175 g) sungold tomatoes, halved
1 tsp. (4 g) minced shallots
Tomato water (recipe below)
8 tomato "petals" (recipe below)
Salt and white pepper

Preheat oven to 275°F (135°C).

Mix butter and miso together at room temperature. Spread evenly over each piece of fish. Place the fish on a buttered sauté pan and into the preheated oven for 7 minutes.

Sauté halved fairytale eggplant and diced Italian eggplant in olive oil in a medium sauté pan over medium heat for about 5 minutes. Add 1 Tbsp. of the white balsamic, miso, and mirin, and deglaze, cooking for 5 minutes.

Separately, dress sungold tomatoes with minced shallots and the remaining 1 Tbsp. of white balsamic.

In a small saucepan, gently warm the tomato water over low heat. Pour into serving bowls and add a mound of sautéed eggplant. Float sungold tomatoes in the tomato water. Add cooked fish on top of the eggplant mixture. Top the fish with a tomato petal. Serve.

Tomato Water

Yields 1 qt (1 L)

4 medium beefsteak tomatoes, cut into large chunks
Pulp from making tomato "petals"
1 clove garlic

Chop tomatoes (with the pulp left over from making tomato petals) and garlic in a food processor. Place a fine mesh sieve in a large bowl, and line with cheesecloth. Place chopped tomatoes and garlic in the cheesecloth-lined sieve, and allow to drain, refrigerated, overnight.

Reserve the collected liquid and discard the solids.

Tomato "Petals"

Yields 8 pcs.

4 Roma tomatoes
1 Tbsp. olive oil
½ tsp. salt

Score a cross into the skin of the tomatoes opposite the stem, blanch them, shock in ice water and peel. Remove the pulp and ribs inside of the tomatoes (and reserve for tomato water) and cut the remaining fleshy part in half to make two large petal shapes per tomato. Season petals with olive oil and salt in a bowl.

Lay seasoned petals on a parchment-lined sheet tray. Cook in a 120°F (50°C) oven for two hours until concentrated.

DUCK BREAST WITH CORN, PEPPERS AND WINE BERRIES

An umami combo of duck, corn and peppers. Served on a yellow sauce of corn purée and surrounded by edible wildflowers and wine berries, this dish also rates high on vibrant visual appeal.

SERVES 4

- 4 boneless duck breasts
- 2 Tbsp. butter
- 2 sprigs thyme
- 2 cloves garlic
- 2 cups (350 g) corn kernels
- 1 cup (175 g) mixed bell peppers, cut into matchsticks
- 2 Tbsp. (26 g) pickled peppers, cut into matchsticks (recipe below)
- 2 Tbsp. (26 g) cipollini onions, peeled and cut into small crescents
- ½ cup (125 g) corn purée (recipe below)
- 1 tsp. jalapeno peppers, minced
- ½ cup (80 g) wine berries, washed

Cooking the duck

Season duck breasts and cook skin-side down in a large sauté pan on medium-low heat until crisp. Add butter, garlic and thyme to the pan and baste flesh side for 20 seconds.

Remove the duck from the pan and allow to rest for up to 20 minutes.

Cooking the corn mix

Sauté cipollini onions in a small sauté pan over medium heat until translucent, about 5 minutes. Add corn kernels, raw pepper slices and raw minced jalapeno. Continue to sauté gently. Add corn purée to bind the vegetables together and season to taste with salt, pepper and lime juice.

Finishing the dish

Lay a small pool of the sauté mix in the center of the dish.

Top with slices of duck breast. Season the breasts with sea salt and black pepper. Finish with thin slices of pickled peppers and raw wine berries

Corn Purée

Yields 1 pt. (480 ml)

- 1 qt. (700 g) corn kernels (reserve corn cobs)
- ½ cup (85 g) onions, peeled and sliced
- 1 tsp. honey
- 2 tsp. lime juice
- Salt to taste

Cut corn cobs in quarters and cover with water in a large sauce pan. Simmer 45 minutes over medium heat and strain, reserving the corn stock. Discard cobs.

In a medium sauce pan over medium heat, sweat onions and corn kernels until tender, about 5 minutes. Add 1 pint (450 ml) of reserved corn stock and simmer for 30 minutes.

Put contents in a blender and blend on high speed until smooth. Pass through a fine-mesh sieve. Season to taste with honey, lime juice and salt

Pickled Peppers

Yields 1 qt. (1 L)

- 1 qt. (700 g) peppers, mixed colors, sliced into matchsticks
- 3 cups (720 ml) rice vinegar
- ⅓ cup (65 g) sugar
- ⅓ cup (80 ml) water
- 1 Tbsp. salt

Bring all ingredients to a simmer except the peppers.

Pour liquid over the peppers and allow to cool to room temperature.

SHIITAKE MUSHROOM LASAGNA WITH SPRING GREENS

Great for vegetarians, this lasagna is sure to satisfy thanks to umami-rich shiitake and other mushrooms, plus cheese.

SERVES 16

Pasta

2¾ cups (345 g) "00" (*doppio zero*) flour
½ cup (80 g) semolina flour
½ tsp. kosher salt
4 large eggs
Cold water, as needed, about ¼ to ⅓ cup (60 to 80 ml)

Combine flours and salt. Pour flour mixture onto clean kitchen counter and mound into a pile. Make a well in the center of the flour. Add eggs to well. With a fork, stir the egg with the flour, starting near the well and slowly working in more and more flour. Add water as needed, until the pasta dough is combined and easily kneaded. Knead by hand until the dough comes together in a smooth ball.

Roll pasta dough by hand or through pasta machine, until about 1/16 in. (1.5 mm) thick. Cut into 4 sheets for layering in the lasagna.

Cook pasta sheets in salted, boiling water for 2 minutes and shock in ice water. Removed from the ice water and lightly coat the sheets with olive oil so they don't stick together.

Filling

1½ lbs. (675 g) shiitake mushrooms, stemmed and sliced
½ lb. (225 g) button mushrooms, stemmed and sliced
1 bunch leeks, white part only, diced
10 cipollini onions, peeled, halved and sliced
2 bunches spring onion, cleaned, greens removed and reserved, whites sliced
4 white onions, peeled, minced
1 qt. (900 ml) béchamel sauce (recipe below)
2 Tbsp. prepared horseradish
2 bunches ramps (wild leeks), cleaned, whites sliced, greens reserved and cut into 1-in. (2.5-cm) ribbons
2 bunches nettles, picked (wear gloves when handling raw nettles)
2 bunches Swiss chard, sliced into ribbons
2 Tbsp. chopped *shiso*
8 oz. (225 g) ricotta, whipped with zest of 1 lemon and 1 Tbsp. olive oil and seasoned with salt and pepper
8 oz. (225 g) goat cheese
8 oz. (225 g) *Grana Padano*, grated
Toasted slivered almonds
capers
spring onions

Preheat oven to 350°F (175°C).

Season mushrooms with olive oil and salt, place on a sheet tray and roast in the oven until golden brown, about 15 minutes.

Grill spring onions and fry capers. Make lemon confit.

In medium sauté pan, over medium heat, sweat cipollini onions, leeks, and spring onions separately until soft, about 5 minutes each, then combine and reserve.

In heavy-bottomed medium saucepan, over medium heat, gently cook minced onions until soft and translucent. Remove half of the cooked minced onions and combine with the reserved onion mixture. Reduce heat to low and continue to cook remaining minced onions until caramelized, about 25 minutes. Once caramelized, combine with the reserved onion mixture. Add béchamel and horseradish to onion mixture and combine. Season with salt and pepper and allow to cool to room temperature.

In a large pot of boiling water, blanch separately the nettles, ramps, spring onion greens and Swiss chard until soft, about 30 seconds to 1 minute each. Remove from boiling water and shock in ice water to retain their bright green color. Slice the nettle leaves into ribbons after blanching and shocking.

Coat the inside of a roasting pan or lasagna pan with olive oil. Lay 1 lasagna sheet, scatter with dollops of ¼ of the onion mixture, ¼ of the blanched greens, ¼ of the roasted mushrooms, ¼ of each cheese, and ¼ of the shiso. Repeat to build 4 layers.

Bake for 20 to 30 minutes, rotating in the oven halfway through the cooking process.
Remove from oven and garnish with grated Grana Padano, fried capers, toasted slivered almonds, roasted shiitake mushrooms and grilled spring onions.

Béchamel Sauce

¼ lb. (115 g) butter
¾ cup (80 g) flour
1 qt. (900 ml) milk
Nutmeg

Melt butter in a small stock pot or Dutch oven over medium heat. Slowly whisk flour into the butter, and allow to cook gently over low heat for 8 to 10 minutes, being careful not to burn it. Slowly whisk milk into butter/flour mixture. When the mixture thickens and begins to bubble, remove from heat and season with salt, pepper and freshly grated nutmeg.

DAVID KIN

I first encountered the concept of umami when I was working in New York as a young cook. Tasting dashi, it is hard to find and describe umami because it is not an overt sensation like taste and smell. It's much more subtle and refined.

When I later became a chef in my own restaurants, umami became an important factor for the balance of flavors in all of my dishes. This was a gradual process, because it took a long time to really understand. An understanding of umami increases the understanding of creating balance in a dish, which is very important when you're trying to make something delicious and satisfying.

For me important umami ingredients include dashi and shiitake mushrooms. A dried shiitake has the easiest-to-understand umami, because there's a distinctive concentration effect in the dried shiitake. What's wonderful about dashi is not only the strong umami properties but also its subtlety and delicacy, so you can do anything with it—even incorporate dashi into western-style dishes. I use dashi as a seasoning and a base which serves as a versatile blank slate, delicately infusing all sorts of dishes. A very important thing about umami is the synergy between ingredients. I emphasize this because if the kombu equals one and the *katsuobushi* (dried bonito flakes) equals one, when you put them together then it's NOT two, its FOUR or FIVE. The combination of them has a synergistic quality. If you take this combination, then add dried shiitake mushrooms, it's even more…it's exponential.

The combination of parmesan with cooked tomato is the western equivalent of katsuobushi and kombu together. Aged parmesan contains a lot of umami. I've found the rind contains a lot of umami also.

In the past 5 years in my cooking I have been trying to use a little bit less fat and make it more healthy. I want it to be incredibly delicious, exciting, and colorful. A lot of times in western cooking flavor and deliciousness comes from fat. I'm trying to reduce the fat, so I have to look for other ways to add that savoriness or that deliciousness. That is where umami becomes very important. Umami is one of the steps on the ladder to deliciousness, layer upon layer giving complexity and flavor.

CH

Manresa Los Gatos

LOVE APPLE FARMS TOMATOES WITH PARMESAN

Manresa partners with local Love Apple Farms to use their vegetables in its cooking. Seductively sweet cherry tomatoes combine with a soup extracted from the rind of umami-rich parmesan to create an exquisite umami hit for the palate.

SERVES up to 6–8

Parmesan Consommé

480 g (17 oz.) Parmigiano Reggiano, cut into 1-in. (2.5-cm) chunks
15 g *Rishiri* kombu
960 g vegetable stock
Champagne vinegar, to taste
0.2% xanthan gum

Combine all ingredients in pressure cooker and cook on high pressure for 20 minutes. Strain liquid through cheesecloth and allow to cool to room temperature. Adjust the seasoning with salt if needed and add a touch of acidity to taste with the vinegar. Weigh the liquid and place in blender. On low speed, shear in 0.2% of the liquid's weight in xanthan gum for 2 minutes or until the gum is fully hydrated. Strain through cheesecloth one more time.

Tomatoes

1 kg (2 lbs.) cherry tomatoes, assorted sizes and colors.
Olive oil
Maldon sea salt

Pick off the green stems of the cherry tomatoes. Blanch the tomatoes in boiling water in small batches, about 10 at a time, for exactly 10 seconds and plunge into ice water immediately. Peel the tomatoes and keep whole. Place the tomatoes in a shallow pan and season with extra virgin olive oil. Make sure to coat the entire surface of the tomatoes.

To serve

To plate, lift the tomatoes out of the oil and drain them of excess oil. Arrange them nicely in a bowl with the stem side down. Pour the parmesan consommé over and around the tomatoes until it comes halfway up the sides of the tomatoes. Garnish the tomatoes with small basil leaves and a few grains of Maldon sea salt. Serve at room temperature.

SUMMER CLAMS, PEAS AND BEANS IN A PINE MUSHROOM BROTH

Kombu, *matsutake* mushrooms, and dried tuna flakes (*maguro bushi*) combine in a superb example of umami synergism in stock. On top of that, copious umami is extracted from the clams.

SERVES 8

Clams

2.75 kg (6 lbs.) cherrystone clams and Wellfleet clams
40 g (1½ oz.) *Rishiri* kombu
2 qts. water

Place cold water and kombu into a large pot. Add the clams to the pot and place on high heat covered with a lid. Once the liquid comes to a boil, the clams will open shortly after. Remove the clams from the liquid and shuck them from their shells. Trim off the "skirt" so that only the "meat" remains. Strain the liquid and store the clams submerged in just enough strained liquid to cover them and keep them hydrated.

Geoduck

1 live geoduck clam
Olive oil

Cut off the trunk of the clam. Open the shell and remove the meaty skirt off the inside of the geoduck. Clean out the neck and body of all sand by rinsing well in cold running water. Blanch each piece for 10 seconds in boiling water, then plunge into ice water. When chilled, peel off the membrane. Slice thinly and sear on a *plancha* (a flat, Spanish-style griddle) with olive oil for a few seconds.

Pickled Kelp

230 g (230 ml) rice wine vinegar
230 g (230 ml) white wine vinegar
230 g (230 ml) water
½ cup plus 2 tsp. sugar
110 g (4 oz.) *battera* kombu, rinsed in cold water and cut crosswise into ¾-in. (2-cm) strips (3 servings per piece)

Whisk the vinegars, water and sugar together and boil until all the sugar is dissolved. Cool the mixture to room temperature. Submerge the kelp in the pickling liquid, cover and steep overnight in the refrigerator. The pickled kelp can be made ahead of time and will keep for months.

Dashi

1.8 L (2 qts.) filtered water
12 g (⅓ oz.) dried shiitake mushrooms
15 g (½ oz.) dried large kombu
25 g (⅔ oz.) dried tuna flakes (*magurobushi*)
75 g (4 to 5 Tbsp., or to taste) white soy sauce (*shiro shoyu*)
Sea salt

Combine the water, mushrooms, and kelp in a large pan and heat to 140°F (60°C). Turn off the heat, cover the pan and steep for 1 hour. Remove and discard the kelp. Heat the mushrooms and broth to 175°F (80°C). Add the tuna shavings, stir for 15 seconds and immediately strain through a linen cloth. Discard the solids and season the broth to taste with white soy sauce and salt. If making ahead, reserve in the refrigerator.

Matsutake

450 g whole *matsutake* mushrooms

Clean the mushrooms thoroughly with a damp cloth. Cut them in half. Bring 1 L (1.1 qts.) of dashi to a simmer and gently poach the mushrooms in the dashi until done, about 5 minutes. Cut each mushroom half into attractive bite-sized pieces and set aside. Strain the dashi and reserve.

To serve

1 to 2 sheets gold-grade nori, toasted and torn into 1- to 2-in. pieces
Green scallion tops, sliced very thin on an extreme bias and soaked in ice water to curl
Peas, blanched and double shucked
Pole beans, shaved very thin and soaked in ice water to curl
1 to 2 whole *yuzu*

Place nori, a spoonful of peas, the clams and the matsutake mushrooms in bowl and pour simmering hot dashi over them to cover. Place scallions, shaved beans and pickled kelp in broth. With a microplane, zest a small amount of yuzu on the surface of the soup. Serve immediately.

MILK PANNA COTTA WITH ABALONE

The umami in abalone exuded during braising is reduced to a jelly. Mixing it into the base of *yuzu* panna cotta as you eat creates delicate flavor harmony.

SERVES up to 20

Braised abalone

450 to 680 g (1 to 1.5 lbs.) abalone in shell, scrubbed
1 L (1 qt.) water
½ cup (100 ml) sake
½ tsp. salt
50 to 60 g (¼ cup) *usukuchi* soy sauce

Place abalone in pot of cold salted water and bring to a boil. As soon as the water boils, take the abalone out of the water, remove it from the shell and trim off the viscera. In a clean pot, combine cleaned abalone, sake, water and salt. Simmer for approximately 3 hours, skimming when necessary. Remove from heat and season to taste with soy sauce, beginning with 3 Tbsp. and adding more if necessary. Reserve about 3 cups (750 ml) cooking liquid for abalone jelly. Refrigerate abalone in enough remaining liquid so it can marinate, absorbing more flavor. Before serving, slice abalone very thinly, cut the slices into randomly shaped small pieces (about ½ in.) and toss with dressing (recipe below).

Milk panna cotta

½ cup (120 ml) cream
1½ cups (590 ml) milk
10 g bronze-grade sheet gelatin
3 g salt
1 Tbsp. plus 2 tsp. (25 ml) *yuzu* juice

Rehydrate gelatin in ice water, strain and remove as much water as possible. Heat cream to 140°F (60°C), melt gelatin into cream and stir until fully dissolved. Add cream to milk, then season with kosher salt and yuzu juice. Adjust seasoning if necessary. With a small ladle, spoon a measured portion (about 30 ml) into individual laquerware serving dishes. Refrigerate on a level surface for at least one hour.

Abalone jelly

13.5 g silver-grade sheet gelatin
About 3 cups (750 ml) cooking liquid

Rehydrate gelatin in ice water, strain and remove as much water as possible. Heat abalone liquid to 140°F (60°C), melt gelatin into liquid and stir until fully dissolved. Pour liquid into a metal bowl over an ice bath. While stirring, cool to 40°F (5°C), then gently ladle a measured portion (about 1.3 oz.) of jelly over the set panna cotta. Refrigerate on a level surface until completely set.

Abalone dressing

½ cup (100 ml) *shiro* dashi
½ cup (100 ml) olive oil

To serve

Breakfast radishes, shaved into paper thin slices
Baby radishes, whole or quartered
Salad burnet, separated into individual leaves
Extra virgin olive oil
Fleur de sel

Arrange 7 to 10 dressed abalone pieces on top of each individual dish of set jelly. Garnish each serving with 5 to 7 radish slices, 1 to 2 pieces of baby radish, 7 to 9 salad burnet leaves, a drizzle of olive oil and a few grains of salt.

FIRE ROASTED EGGPLANT WITH SQUID CARAMEL

Fragrant grilled eggplant is cloaked in an umami-rich sauce of *katsuobushi* and soy sauce, with a homemade *furikake* (sprinkles normally eaten with rice) of seaweed and grains adding a delightful crispiness.

SERVES 8

Grilled Eggplant

2 whole eggplants, 250 g (about 9 oz.) each

Blister the skin of the eggplants over a hot wood fire. When the skin is charred, but the flesh is still somewhat firm, wrap the eggplants in foil and set them aside for ½ hour to finish cooking from the residual heat. Open the foil packet and remove the skin. Cut each eggplant in quarters, lengthwise.

Charred Squid

Clean and eviscerate squid, then soak in milk until you are ready to cook. Drain off milk and sear quickly with high heat on a *plancha* or grill pan, turning occasionally until carmelized. Season with salt to finish.

Bonito Soy Sauce

100 g *koikuchi* soy sauce
100 g ponzu
10 g (⅓ oz.) bonito flakes

Heat the soy and ponzu just to a simmer. Add the bonito flakes, remove from heat, cover, and steep for one hour. Strain and reserve the flavored soy sauce.

Squid Caramel

Olive oil
4 onions, sliced thinly
450 g (1 lb.) cleaned squid, cut into rings
1 qt. (1 L) vegetable stock
Ground *kudzu* starch

Sweat down onions in pan with just enough olive oil to coat and let stew until soft and caramelized golden brown. Add squid and cook down until it releases liquid. Continue to cook and let the juices reduce down. Add the vegetable stock and reduce down until you reach a viscous consistency with an amber color. Strain through chinois and whisk in 50% kudzu starch to the weight of the liquid. Strain once more and season with salt to taste.

Eggplant Chips

1 eggplant, 250 g (about 9 oz.)
Extra virgin olive oil
Kosher salt

Line a large sheet pan with a silicone baking mat brushed with olive oil and preheat an oven to 285°F (140°C). If you have a convection oven, set the fan to low. Cut the eggplant in half lengthwise and slice the halves on a mandolin set at about 1⁄16 in. Place at least 8 slices on the oiled mat, brush olive oil on top of each slice, and season the eggplant lightly with salt. Cover the slices with another silicon baking mat, and bake at 285°F (140°C) for 10 minutes. Reduce the oven temperature to 275°F (135°C), turn the pan, and bake for another 10 minutes. Allow the chips to cool and hold in a dry box.

Furikake

45 g (1½ oz.) delicata squash seeds, cleaned and dehydrated overnight
20 g (⅔ oz.) wild rice
1 L grapseed oil for frying
40 small leaves Toscano kale
2 g nutritional yeast
Kosher salt
Olive oil
20 g (⅔ oz.) gold-grade *nori*, toasted over low heat
30 g (1 oz.) dried kombu
10 g (⅓ oz.) freshly shaved *katsuobushi*
45 g (1½ oz.) white sesame seeds, lightly toasted
10 g (⅓ oz.) black sesame seeds, lightly toasted

Heat grapeseed oil to 390°F (200°C) and fry wild rice from raw until puffed, drain and cool. Then let the oil cool down to 325°F (160°C) and fry the delicata seeds until golden and crispy. Drain and cool. Toss kale leaves in just enough olive oil to coat them and season with kosher salt and nutritional yeast. Lay out on silpat and place another silpat on top. Bake at 275° F (130°C) (if using a convection oven, set fan to low), turning every 5 minutes until crispy. Pulverize wild rice with mortar and pestle to crumbs. In a spice grinder, pulse the kale chips until uniform pieces. Then tear the nori and pulse in the spice grinder the same way as the kale. Chop the dried kombu lightly. In a large bowl, mix everything well with gloved hands and check seasoning, adjust with kosher salt if necessary.

To Serve

Place one spoonful of the squid caramel on the plate and drag with spoon to mimic the shape and size of the eggplant. Dress each eggplant quarter with the bonito soy, top with a thin layer of furikake mix, and place on top of the caramel. Finish with pieces of the charred squid and top with an eggplant chip.

Modern approaches to umami in Nordic cuisine

The New Nordic cuisine and Nordic Food Lab

The New Nordic Cuisine, as defined in a manifesto in 2004, was established to express the purity, freshness, simplicity, and ethics that Nordic populations would associate with their own terroir. The manifesto elaborates on several points, including (i) uncomplicated preparations that bring out the flavors of the raw materials—food that can be both rustic and elegant—and (ii) honest food: that is, food made without superfluous exertions, complications, manipulations, or transformations. For these reasons, the New Nordic Cuisine, spearheaded by chef René Redzepi and his acclaimed restaurant *noma*, resonates widely in the Nordic countries and internationally.

Experimentation at Nordic Food Lab in Copenhagen studying deliciousness in old and new raw materials using both old and new processes.

Nordic Food Lab was born out of the impulse to research these points further. Established in 2008 as an independent non-profit organization, it was made as a place where chefs, scientists, academics, and producers could collaborate to explore the building blocks of Nordic food and share the results from this work with other chefs, the food industry, and the general public. From a small houseboat in Copenhagen harbor, an international team of chefs and scientists investigate old and new raw materials and techniques, seeking out the roots of deliciousness of Nordic ingredients.

The lab functions as a kitchen where the chefs' intuition and experience are combined with scientific knowledge and methods, using a systematic approach to exploring deliciousness. Some of the lab's projects have employed lactic and acetic acid fermentation and enzymatic breakdown; catalogued wild edible plants for diversifying flavors; investigated umami and how to employ it in the kitchen; and studied underutilized food resources like seaweeds, insects, and game.

From dulse *dashi*, pork-*bushi, peaso*, and barley *tempeh*—to mackerel and grasshopper *garum*

Some projects at Nordic Food Lab involve both traditional and new raw materials and methods to create foods that are rich in umami. In many cases this work has

Ole G. Mouritsen
Professor Ph.D. DSc, University of Southern Denmark and Nordic Food Lab

Josh Evans, Ben Reade, and
Michael Bom Frøst, Nordic Food Lab

Umami-rich products from Nordic Food Lab: Top: samples of fermented fish *garum*. Middle: pork-*bushi*. Bottom: fried fermented pearl barley, a Nordic interpretation of *tempeh*.

been inspired by ancient Japanese approaches involving seaweeds, fermentation using *kōji* (traditionally used in *sake*, *miso*, and *shoyu* production), as well as aging methods similar to *katsuobushi* production.

Developing new and diverse sources of umami is a central pursuit at the lab. This work has given rise to all sorts of discoveries: dashi made from red dulse (a kind of seaweed), pork-*bushi*, *peaso* and other *miso*-like pastes, as well as *garums* and fermented sauces made with herring, mackerel, grasshoppers, and other proteinaceous substrates. In the quest for umami synergy, the lab has implemented the traditional Japanese techniques for *katsuobushi* production by fermenting hot-smoked, dried lean pig muscle. The resulting "pork-*bushi*" has a pleasant smell and taste, similar to Parma ham. Other fermented products using *kōji*, a grain substrate colonized by the mold *Aspergillus orzyae*, include a kind of Nordic *tempeh* or fermented cake of pearl barley, and *peaso*, a *miso*-like product based on split yellow peas. Fermentation of fresh fish such as mackerel using its own intestinal enzymes has resulted in a Nordic version of the classical Roman fish sauce, *garum*, which is a rich source of umami. Recently the lab has focused on fermenting insects, developing new umami-rich products that bring previously inedible substances into the realm of the edible through delicious taste. One such product is a grasshopper *garum* fermented with barley *koji*.

Literature

J. Evans, "Non-trivial pursuit—new approaches to Nordic deliciousness," *Anthropology of Food*, S7 (2012), http://aof.revues.org/7262.

M. E. Hermansen, "Creating terroir—An anthropological perspective on New Nordic Cuisine as an expression of Nordic identity," *Anthropology of Food*, S7 (2012), http://aof.revues.org/7249.

J. Risbo, O.G. Mouritsen, M. B. Frøst, J. D. Evans & B. Reade, "Culinary science in Denmark: Molecular gastronomy and beyond," *J. Culinary Sci. Technol.* 11, 111–130 (2013).

SO AME

VIRGILIO MARTINEZ

Central Lima

UTHI RICA

PEDRO MIGUEL SCHIAFFINO

Malabar Lima

When I met umami for the first time, I was very little, about 10 years old. This occurred in the north coast of Peru when I ate ceviche with tomato and raw shrimp (it is strange and very different from a typical Peruvian ceviche. I was very close to the border with Ecuador). I assumed it had something to do with the mixing of flavors and from the very ripe tomato sauce and the shrimp broth.

I experienced a very intense deliciousness, but didn't know how to describe it. Since then shrimp and tomatoes hold a special place in my memory. The umami taste for me is mouthwatering, somehow you start to feel a nice heaviness and depth in your mouth, full of a meaty sensation. It feels meaty…without depending on meat products.

As a chef, discovering the umami taste changed my way of thinking about cooking. I now think more about using seaweeds, intensity of flavors, giving more flavor, going a bit further. But always with a sense of balance, to create a sense of taste that is on a different level from normal flavors. That's the importance of coping with improvisation: you get to adapt recipes to different understandings, with global or local foods. Designing different things using improvisation. Using this knowledge creates an experience.

There are some particular ingredients which contain umami in Peru. We have some very interesting mushrooms in the Andes, and tree tomatoes in the Amazon of Peru. Also, while you can get many Peruvian ingredients anywhere in the world, the really good ones are here, such as fish, tomatoes and fruit. This is what makes Peruvian food so adaptable to many other places throughout the world.

I play with umami a lot more in cold preparations to enhance the taste of raw seafood with just a little seasoning, using the taste of the product to my advantage. For example, raw scallops are served rolled in *kanihua*, a typical Andean cereal similar to quinoa. My ceviche's *leche de tigre* contains *tumbo*, a banana-shaped passion fruit that extracts the sweetness of the fresh scallops.

As long we continue asking and looking for the truth in food, we will discover that a lot more is driven by umami flavor motivation. What I mean is that umami is really, really delicious; it challenges us to look for new processes and new discoveries. We need to continue our search for more ingredients hidden in unknown parts of the world. There is umami in the Amazon and in the Andes. When we discover new expressions of umami in new products, it's just fantastic.

VIRGILIO MARTINEZ

Central Lima

SCALLOPS, RED KIWICHA, TUMBO FRUIT EMULSION

Kiwicha (amaranth) is an ancient Peruvian plant popular recently for its high nutrient value. This recipe uses both red kiwicha and kiwicha leaves, accompanied by a sauce made from *tumbo*, a variety of passionfruit. A dish of superlatively balanced umami and tang.

SERVES 4

8 scallops
Kiwicha leaves

Tumbo tiger's milk

2⅔ oz. (80 g) white onion
2 oz. (60 g) celery
1 tsp. garlic
1 tsp. ginger
2 Tbsp. lime juice
2 tsp. cilantro
¼ cup (70 ml) *tumbo* juice
1 Tbsp. plus 1 tsp. *porcon* mushroom "juice"

Liquefy the onion, celery, ginger, and garlic, then pass through a sieve. Add the lime juice, tumbo juice, cilantro leaves and porcon mushroom "juice" (hydrate dried porcon in water, remove and bring to a boil in new water, reduce for 1 hour and strain). Marinate for 20 minutes, then remove the cilantro.

Red kiwicha:

2 oz. (60 g) red *kiwicha*
⅔ cup (150 ml) coral broth

Make a broth by sautéing the reserved scallop coral, adding water and simmering for 20 minutes. You will need at least 1½ cups (350 ml) of coral broth all together. Cook the kiwicha in ⅔ cup (150 ml) of the broth for 8 minutes.

Crunchy kiwicha:

⅔ oz. (20 g) red *kiwicha*
1⅔ oz. (50 g) overcooked white rice
¾ cup (200 ml) coral broth

Cook the kiwicha in ¼ cup (50 ml) of coral broth as in the previous preparation. Combine the cooked kiwicha with the overcooked white rice and the remaining coral broth and liquefy in a blender. Pass through a sieve, spread thinly out on a silicone baking mat and place in the oven for 10 minutes.

Clean the scallops and set apart the coral (roe). Slice scallops and keep cold.

Reserve some fresh kiwicha leaves for garnish. Dehydrate the rest of the leaves in a 190°F (90°C) oven for 4 hours. Grind the dehydrated leaves into a powder.

Place the scallops on the plate, add the kiwicha on top so it seems to be the coral of the scallop, place dots of the tumbo fruit emulsion around the scallops and decorate with the crunchy kiwicha.

CHARRED OCTOPUS, PURPLE CORN, SEAWEED

Both the seaweed *cochayuyo* and purple corn are integral to Peruvian gastronomy. Here corn sprouts are steeped in a clam dashi. Served with fragrant grilled octopus, the result is umami of marvelous depth.

SERVES 8 to 10

2½ lbs. (1.2 kg) octopus
⅔ oz. (20 g) corn silk

Purple corn reduction

4 ears purple corn
3½ oz. (100 g) *cochayuyo* seaweed
1⅓ oz. (40 g) garlic
½ cup (100 ml) olive oil

Slow-cook the garlic in the olive oil to make garlic confit. Add the purple corn and cochayuyo, let infuse for 1 hour, then pass through a sieve and reduce for 30 minutes. Liquefy the garlic and the purple corn/cochayuyo reduction.

Sprout emulsion

10 oz. (300 g) corn sprouts
½ cup (100 ml) clam broth
1 oz. (30 g) garlic
½ cup (100 ml) olive oil

Make garlic confit with the olive oil. Blanch the sprouts and make an emulsion with the clam broth (make the clam broth by any traditional method), garlic confit and olive oil.

Corn powder

7 oz. (200 g) multicolored *cancha* corn
2 Tbsp. purple corn juice

Sauté the multicolored cancha corn until it pops and jumps. Grind into a coarse powder and color with only a few drops of purple corn juice.

Cook the octopus by any traditional method.

Fry the corn silk in 400°F (200°C) oil for 5 seconds.

Squeeze out the purple corn reduction in dots, place pieces of the charred octopus on the top of the dots, decorate the plate with more purple dots so they seem to form the tentacles of the octopus, and make a splash with the sprout emulsion using a spoon.

VIRGILIO MARTINEZ

OCA, CUSHURO, CAÑIHUA AND TREE TOMATO

*O*ca is a yam cultivated on the Andean plateau. Drying makes it sweeter, hence the confit. The *sachatomate* or tree tomato is indeed very like a tomato in appearance but is a fruit, rich in both umami and sweetness.

SERVES 4

4 *oca* tubers
2 Tbsp. (25 ml) olive oil for cooking oca
3½ oz. (100 g) *cushuro*
1 Tbsp. olive oil for dressing cushuro
2 oz. (60 g) *cañihua*
Cañihua leaves
Oxalis flowers

Tree tomato emulsion

5 *sachatomate* (tree tomatoes)
1 oz. (30 g) garlic
½ cup (100 ml) olive oil

Cook oca in olive oil in a vacuum bag at 185°F (85°C) for 45 minutes. Dress cushuro with olive oil. Cook cañihua in boiling water for 8 minutes. Keep warm.

To make the tree tomato emulsion, first peel and deseed the tree tomatoes and cut them open into "tomato petals." Roast them in an oven for 30 minutes at 300°F (150°C). Slow-cook the garlic in the olive oil to make confit. Purée the roasted tree tomato "petals" and garlic confit and emulsify with the olive oil used in the confit.

Dehydrate the cañihua leaves in an oven for 4 hours at 195°F (90°C).

With a spoon, draw lines of the tree tomato emulsion on the center of the dish, place the ocas on the top of the lines and arrange the cushuro and cañihua like a little garden.

LAMB, LAKE TITICACA ALGAE, CANCHA AND "MILK"

Cancha is the Peruvian version of popcorn, oven-baked to crunchy perfection. Combine with tender milk-fed lamb and sheep's milk cheese for a tempting contrast of textures.

SERVES 4

1 lb. (400 to 500 g) leg of lamb
1 Tbsp. plus 1 tsp. olive oil

Crunchy cancha

7 oz. (200 g) fresh corn
1⅔ oz. (50 g) *aji amarillo* paste
1½ cup (350 ml) vegetable broth
5 oz. (150 g) tapioca powder
1 oz. (30 g) *cancha* corn

Paper Milk

600 g sheep's milk (must be weighed for accuracy)
4 g kappa carrageenan
8 g iota carrageenan
56 g cream cheese

Demiglace

1⅔ oz. (50 g) Lake Titicaca algae

Cook the leg of lamb with the olive oil in a vacuum bag for 17 hours at 160°F (70°C).

Sauté the fresh corn with the aji amarillo paste, then add the vegetable broth and cook for 15 minutes. Liquefy into a paste. Mix the paste with tapioca powder and cook for 20 more minutes. Pass through a sieve and spread out on a silicone baking mat. Place in a 195°F (90°C) oven for 10 minutes.

Mix kappa and iota carrageenans, then add to the sheep's milk and heat over a low flame. Add the cream cheese and stir for a few minutes. Place into molds until set, then cut into small cubes.

Reduce all cooking juices from the lamb. Add the algae and let infuse.

Serve the lamb glazed with the demiglace and decorate the top with the paper milk and the crunchy cancha.

Malabar Lima

PEDRO MIGUEL SCHIAFFINO

I first heard about umami when I met Chef Toshiro Konishi eight years ago. At first I did not pay much attention to it, and I could not really understand it. However, five years later, after I traveled to the Umami Information Center in Tokyo, Japan, I felt I could better understand umami. Umami is a flavor that every cook should keep in mind. We are always thinking about ways to enhance and balance food, and umami provides that: deep flavor and harmony. By combining umami ingredients, food becomes tastier and healthier. Traditional western cuisine has taught us that animal fat equals flavor. Understanding umami belies that statement. It's an important essence to achieve both flavor and balance.

The simple fact of being aware of umami is transforming my cuisine. Today I look for and combine Peruvian ingredients that are rich in glutamate, inosinate and guanylate when conceiving a dish, with the idea of achieving the maximum umami. In Peruvian cuisine, fermented products like corn and *yuca* are important. I believe that some of these fermented products have umami. To showcase the vast pantry of Amazonian cuisine, we had to build our own cuisine, which utilizes unique ingredients like tree tomatoes, *yuca,* and the Amazonian fish *paiche* in a creative manner. Such recipes are inspired by neighboring Amazonian cuisines.

Many Peruvian ingredients are unique and new to the culinary world. There is no reference on how to use them. And of course, we don't know for sure if they are rich in umami. We use our common sense when we cook, and we can mostly determine which ones are rich in umami by association with other ingredients. For example, we have an indigenous type of wild tomato, and we know that if we dry it we will concentrate glutamic acid. When we replace regular tomatoes with the wild dried ones, and we discover that the flavor is enhanced. We can repeat this process with other new ingredients. Still, I think further research about umami in local ingredients is necessary.

I'm always thinking about which of the ingredients that I'm using contain umami. Now, by combining Peruvian umami ingredients and understanding them, I can come up with dishes that are unique, but still balanced and full of rich flavor. As a chef, there were many changes in my thinking when it came to cooking and the creation of dishes after discovering umami. I'd like to introduce the use of umami to the food at my restaurant by looking for local ingredients that have umami, and combining them to obtain an overall balanced flavor.

3000 METERS ABOVE SEA LEVEL

Cushuro is a precious algae-like food discovered in the Andean highlands. More than just a local curiosity, it is rich in umami. It is combined with maca root (*Lepidium meyenii*), wild oca (*Oxalis tuberosa*), wild cucumber and wild celery, all found in the Peruvian Andes. A tangy *leche de tigre* sauce full of umami brings the whole dish together.

SERVES 2

1⅓ oz. (40 g) fresh Andean wild cucumber, blanched
⅓ oz. (10 g) fresh *maca* root, grated
1 oz. (30 g) fresh *cushuro*
⅓ oz. (10 g) wild celery, julienned
⅓ oz. (10 g) wild *Oxalis* tuberosa

⅔ cup (160 ml) *leche de tigre* (recipe below)
1 Tbsp. plus 1 tsp. extra virgin olive oil
Ice cube
Maras salt

Parsley oil

½ cup (100 ml) olive oil
1 tsp. garlic
⅓ oz. (10 g) anchovy filets
2 oz. (60 g) parsley

First combine all the ingredients of the parsley oil in a blender and purée until smooth. Pass through a fine sieve. Combine the leche de tigre in a blender with the parsley oil and emulsify. Place in the refrigerator to keep cold. Before serving add an ice cube to lower the temperature even more.

Season the Andean wild cucumber with Maras salt and olive oil. Do the same with the julienned celery.

Assemble the dish by combining all the vegetables in a deep dish. Add the parsley oil and leche de tigre emulsion. Finish with a few drops of olive oil.

Leche de tigre

SERVES 4

1 small *limo* chili pepper, no veins, chopped
10 oz. (300 g) red onions, roughly chopped
4 cilantro sprigs
3½ oz. (100 g) white fish meat, clean
3½ oz. (100 g) celery, chopped
1 tsp. grated ginger
2 small garlic clove
2 cups (480 ml) fresh squeezed lime juice
2 tsp. *hondashi*
½ tsp. ground pepper
Salt
4 ice cubes

Combine all vegetables and aromatics in a bowl. Season with salt and pepper. Add the fish meat, ice cubes and hondashi, season with salt. Mix well and let rest for 10 minutes. Add the lime juice and mix.

Process everything in a blender, pulse until all vegetables and fish meat are almost a purée.

Pass through a fine sieve and squeeze well, pressing against the sieve, to get out all the juice. Keep cold until used.

GIANT SNAILS WITH CHORIZO AND TURMERIC

These giant Amazonian snails are gathered by an indigenous community near Iquitos and combined with spicy chorizo and sauce into a dish of great flavor depth.

SERVES 2

6 giant Amazonian snails, cleaned
1 oz. (30 g) wild cilantro tapioca
Lime juice

Cooking liquid for the snails

⅔ oz. (20 g) dried tree tomatoes
1 oz. (30 g) roasted tomatoes
2 Tbsp. roasted *aji dulce*
1⅔ oz. (50 g) roasted red onions, chopped
1 tsp. ginger, crushed
1 tsp. fresh turmeric, crushed
1 tsp. garlic, crushed
3½ oz. (100 g) roasted smoked pork bones
1⅔ oz. (50 g) roasted chorizo
2 L fish broth
Fresh wild cilantro

Snake fruit purée

3½ oz. (100 g) fermented snake fruit pulp
⅔ oz. (20 g) coconut oil
1½ Tbsp. coconut milk

Sofrito

1 Tbsp. plus 1 tsp. olive oil
2 tsp. garlic, grated
2 Tbsp. red onion, finely chopped
⅔ oz. (20 g) sweet chili pepper, finely chopped
1 tsp. fresh turmeric, grated
Salt and pepper

Wild cilantro tapioca

1⅔ oz. (50 g) small tapioca pearls
2 cup (500 ml) smoked fish stock
1⅔ oz. (50 g) wild cilantro purée
1⅔ oz. (50 g) cilantro oil
Salt

Place the fish stock in a pot. Season with salt. Boil and add the tapioca. Cook until translucent. Strain and cool down. Add the cilantro purée and oil to the tapioca. Season with salt and keep.

To cook the snails, combine all the ingredients of the cooking liquid, add the snails, bring to a boil and lower the heat. Cook very slowly at 185°F (85°C) until the snails are tender, approximately 4 hours. Take out the snails and keep them covered. Strain the broth through a fine sieve. Reduce the broth to a sauce-like consistency. Add lime juice.

Make the sofrito, cooking it slowly until caramelized.

Make a purée with the snake fruit pulp and coconut milk, then emulsify with the coconut oil. Keep warm.

To serve, place the purée in the bottom of each snail shell, add the snail and top with sofrito. Finish with the reduced cooking liquid and wild cilantro tapioca.

SEA URCHIN AND MUSSELS ON THE SHELL WITH SEAWEED SALAD

A harmony of ocean treasures: sea urchin, mussels and seaweed. The "shells" on which the mussels sit are made from taro root purée. Seaweed adds very few calories but plenty of umami.

SERVES 2

For the sea urchin

2⅓ oz. (70 g) fresh sea urchin
½ cup (120 ml) *leche de tigre* (see p. 89)
2 Tbsp. soy sauce
½ Tbsp. roasted Brazil nut oil
1 tsp. fresh chili pepper, chopped

For the seaweed salad

⅔ oz. (20 g) fresh brown kelp
⅓ oz. (10 g) fresh water lettuce (*Monostroma*) seaweed
⅓ oz. (10 g) fresh red *Porphyra* seaweed
⅔ oz. (20 g) fresh *Chondracanthus* seaweed
⅔ oz. (20 g) tree tomato seeds
⅓ oz. (10 g) fresh oyster leaves
Maras salt

For the dressing

Scant ¼ cup (40 ml) cold smoked pork dashi
1 Tbsp. plus 1 tsp. *leche de tigre* (see p. 89)
1 Tbsp. plus 1 tsp. white wine vinegar
1 Tbsp. soy sauce
⅓ oz. (10 g) sugar, raw

For the mussels on the shell

8 small mussels, cooked
1 oz. (30 g) tomato gelatin (recipe below), diced
⅓ oz. (10 g) seaweed, marinated in dashi
⅔ oz. (20 g) red onion, finely chopped
⅓ oz. (10 g) tobiko
½ oz. (15 g) *leche de tigre* caviar (recipe below)
½ tsp. lime juice

Tomato gelatin
1 cup (240 ml) vine-ripened organic tomato juice
1 tsp. unflavored gelatin
Salt

Place a half cup of tomato juice in a small pot. Add the gelatin and let sit to hydrate. Place the pot an medium heat and cook until the gelatin is dissolved.

Add the rest of the juice and season with salt. Cool down. Place in a square mold and refrigerate until set.

Leche de tigre caviar

About 2 cups (500 g) leche de tigre (see p. 89)
2.5 g sodium alginate (0.5%)
Calcium Chloride Bath
1 L water
5 g calcium chloride

Mix the sodium alginate with the juice using a blender until the sodium alginate is completely dissolved. Strain the mix and store it in the fridge covered in plastic wrap for a few hours to eliminate the air bubbles.

Prepare the calcium bath in a bowl by dissolving the calcium chloride in the water. Use a syringe or a caviar maker to make the caviar. Strain the "caviar" and store in the refrigerator for service

Taro root paste for the "shells"

30 small shells
8⅔ oz. (250 g) taro root purée
1 Tbsp. plus 1 tsp. soy sauce
1 Tbsp. plus 2 tsp. parmesan cheese, grated
¼ cup (60 ml) fish stock
1 tsp. squid ink

To make the "shells," process all the ingredients in a food processor into a smooth paste. Pass them through a fine sieve. Let sit for one night in a cool place. Take the (real) mussel shells and cover each one with plastic wrap. Mix the "shell" paste well and coat the outer part of the real shells with a thin layer of paste. Dehydrate them, then fry in hot oil until crisp.

Season the mussels with salt and lime juice. Add the onions and mix well. Place the mussels on the "shells," add the tomato gelatin, marinated seaweed and tobiko. Finish with "caviar."

Mix all the ingredients for the sea urchin and keep cold.

Blanch all the seaweed for the seaweed salad in fish dashi. Cool them in cold water.

Make the dressing by mixing all ingredients together. Keep cold.

Before serving, mix the seaweed with the dressing, add the oyster leaves and place them in a bowl. Finish with tree tomato seeds and Maras salt.

PEDRO MIGUEL SCHIAFFINO

PAICHE "AJI NEGRO" AND AMAZONIAN ROOTS

An Amazonian freshwater fish, the paiche is a monster, with some specimens growing to over two meters in length. I have gone to the Amazon myself to catch them. Mild in taste, they are easy to eat and ideal in soups and sautés.

SERVES 2

2 fresh paiche, cleaned
4 wild cilantro roots
2 dried *aji dulce*

For the roots

3½ oz. (100 g) sweet corn root (*Calathea allouia*)
1⅔ oz. (50 g) ñame (*Dioscorea trifida*)
1⅔ oz. (50 g) taro root
1⅔ oz. (50 g) coco yam (*Colocasia esculenta*)
1⅔ oz. (50 g) yuca
1 oz. (30 g) wild yuca starch, roasted
1 oz. (30 g) yuca flour, roasted

For the broth

2 cups (480 ml) "aji negro," wild yuca juice
2 cups (480 ml) smoked pork broth
2 fresh *charapita* pepper, crushed
2 fresh sweet chili pepper, crushed
2 leaves fresh wild cilantro
1 tsp. fresh turmeric

Peel the root vegetables and cut them into equal sizes. Place them in a pot with the "aji negro" and smoked pork broth. Bring to a boil, reduce the heat and cook until the roots are tender. Carefully control the doneness of each root—don't overcook them. Take the roots out as they are cooked and reserve. Reserve the broth.

Coat the cooked yuca with roasted yuca flour. Coat the taro root with the roasted wild yuca starch. Keep both warm.

Slice the sweet corn root paper-thin and arrange the slices on top of the paiche filets in a scale pattern. Season with salt. Cook the paiche in a pan with the wild cilantro roots. Keep warm.

Place the aromatics (charapita pepper, sweet pepper, wild cilantro and fresh turmeric) in a cheese cloth. Just before serving, heat the broth, add the aromatics, and simmer for 1 minute. Take out the aromatics and strain the broth.

Place the ñame, taro root, yuca and coco yam in the center of the plate. Place the paiche next to them. Add the hot broth. Finish with the aji dulce and cilantro root.

Dashi from Nordic seaweeds

Kombu: the mother of umami

Japanese *kombu* (*Saccharina japonica*) contains the largest amount of free glutamate known of any foodstuff. When steeped in water for preparing dashi, *kombu* releases some of its glutamate, leading to basal umami. *Nori* from purple laver (*Porphyra yezoensis*), used for wrapping sushi in *maki-zushi* rolls, also contains large amounts of free glutamate, whereas *wakame* (*Undaria pinnatifida*) contains very little and is used in soups more for texture than taste.

In principle, there is no reason why other kinds of seaweed, out of the existing 10,000 different species around the world, could not rival or match *kombu* in producing a good dashi. With this in mind, chefs and scientists in Denmark set out to search for seaweeds, native to the pristine and cold Nordic waters, which could contribute glutamate and hence umami to a Nordic dashi.

Seaweeds in traditional Nordic cuisine

Although it would be expected that populations along the long coastlines of the Nordic countries use seaweeds as food, only Iceland has a historical record of using them in the human diet. In the age when Icelandic sagas were written, dating almost a thousand years back, a particular kind of red seaweed, dulse (*Palmaria palmata*, called *søl* in old Norse) was used as a snack, in soups, and in the classical Icelandic sour-milk product *skyr*. In particular, dried dulse with white spots on the surface (presumably exuded glutamate) was highly prized. Wild sources of dulse are still harvested in Iceland and enter a number of traditional and novel food products.

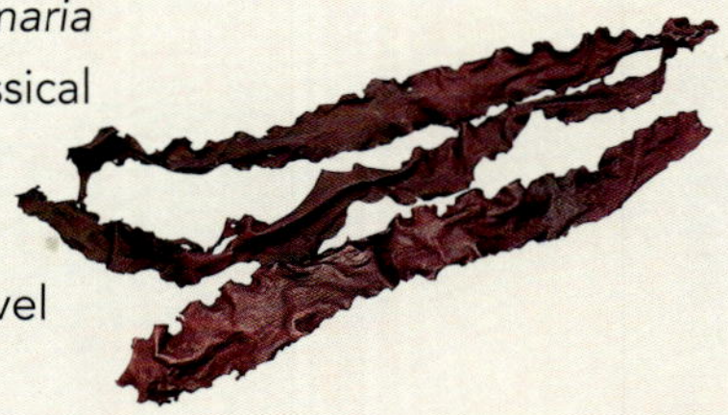

Dulse for Nordic dashi

In recent years, the concept of a New Nordic Cuisine, spearheaded by Restaurant *noma*, has focused on Nordic *terroir* and the use of regional Nordic ingredients of high quality with an aim to enhance taste and promote healthy eating. Inspired by this movement, chefs and scientists associated with Nordic Food Lab set out to explore the potential of Nordic seaweeds, particularly in relation to umami. After tasting combined with chemical analysis, it quickly turned out that dulse, high in glutamate as well as other free amino acids, was an exceptional

A *dashi* made from an extract of dulse.

Ole G. Mouritsen
Professor Ph.D. DSc, University of Southern Denmark and Nordic Food Lab

Some dishes flavored with dulse. From top to bottom: Ice cream without and with infusion with dulse. Fresh cheese infused with dulse. Bread made from a sourdough infused with dulse *dashi*. Veal tartare with dulse.

candidate for creating a dashi with significant umami and interesting sweet and floral notes.

Since its development by Nordic Food Lab, dulse has been used for flavoring different kinds of traditional Nordic dishes. One example is ice cream and fresh cheese (milk curd) that in themselves, being made from cow's milk, have no umami. By infusing the milk used for the ice cream or the fresh cheese with the dulse, more flavorful products have been created that have been received positively by tasters and the general public. Another example is sourdough bread, which has some level of umami caused by the action of the lactic bacteria on the proteins of the flour, but whose taste can be significantly improved by using dulse dashi and chopped dulse instead of water in the dough.

Dried raw dulse can also be used directly in a dish to supply umami, such as in lean veal tartare that has very little flavor of its own, but can be made flavorful by combining with dulse and an emulsion enriched with Worcestershire sauce.

Nordic products for synergistic umami

Nordic Cuisine contains a number of ingredients that can furnish synergistic umami in dashi. Whereas native Nordic fungi like button mushrooms and cepes (porcini) appear to contribute little umami, ingredients like bacon, dried and salted chicken, and shrimp are rich in nucleotides. In particular, smoked and dried heads of small shrimp, as well as cured pork prepared like katsuobushi, provide an interesting Nordic counterpart to Japanese dashi ingredients.

LITERATURE

O.G. Mouritsen, L. Williams, R. Bjerregaard & L. Duelund, "Seaweeds for umami flavour in the New Nordic Cuisine," *Flavour* 1 (2012): 4.

O.G. Mouritsen, *Seaweeds. Edible, Available & Sustainable* (University of Chicago Press, 2013).

O.G. Mouritsen & K. Styrbæk, *Umami. Uncovering the Secrets of the Fifth Taste* (New York Columbia University Press, 2014).

JA

NOBU MATSUHISA

NOBU Tokyo

PAN

YOSHIHIRO MURATA

Kikunoi Kyoto

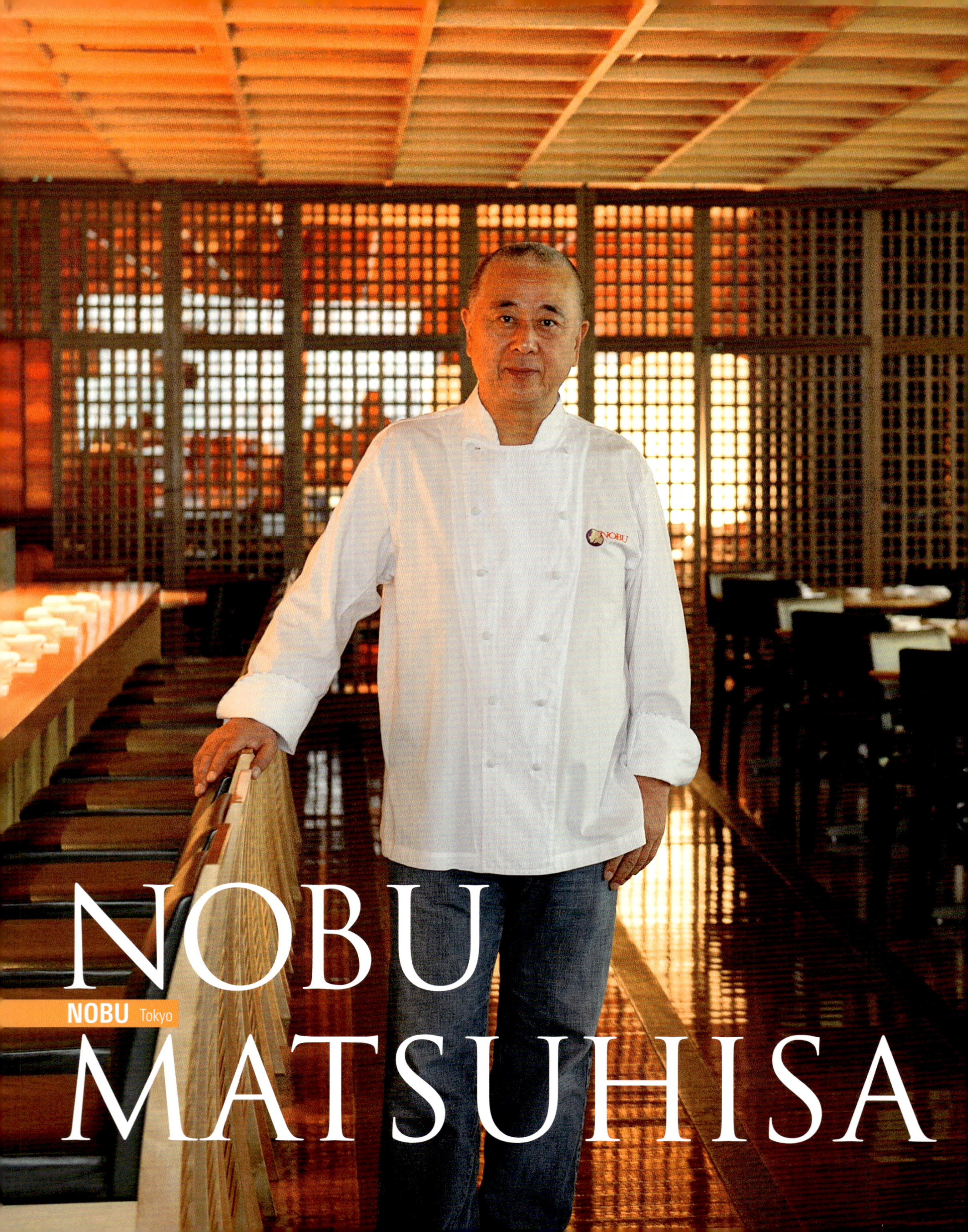

NOBU Tokyo

NOBU MATSUHISA

At all my restaurants, wherever in the world they may be, I focus on serving our guests meals that make the best possible use of local ingredients. In Tokyo, for example, it is easy to buy all sorts of regional foodstuffs shipped to the capital from around Japan, but a chef can obtain much better ingredients by going in person to the areas where they are produced, speaking directly with the producers, and seeing and touching the foods for himself.

Umami was discovered and named by a Japanese scientist, but its sources are by no means limited to specifically Japanese ingredients. It turns up in the local foods of other countries too, offering unexpected discoveries. The *ají* peppers that are popular in Peru are hot, but they also have strong umami. If you add them to sliced onions, the acidity of the onions makes this umami stand out clearly.

When I use umami in my own cooking, I focus on the balance between it and the other four basic tastes (sweet, bitter, sour, and salty). Rather than attempting to make umami stand out, I present it in combination with other tastes, such as sourness and sweetness.

Needless to say, umami is an indispensable element of Japanese cuisine. In my own cooking I am always conscious of the need to include something that says "Japan." Also, I look for culinary synergies. We know, for example, that adding just a dash of salt brings out the sweetness of *an* (sweet bean paste). Taking umami as the base, I seek combinations of tastes that balance as a whole, creating flavors with multidimensional depth.

Umami has long been an element of other countries' cuisines as well, even if it was not explicitly recognized. Examples include dried scallops, *Jinhua* ham, and cheese. I have arrived at my current style of cooking by experimenting with various ways of tapping into this basic taste. I intend to continue presenting umami through my food, and by taking advantage of distinctive local ingredients and flavors, share it with people around the world.

NOBU MATSUHISA

EGG AND DASHI CUSTARD WITH YUBA AND UMEBOSHI

Tomatoes are an accessible source of umami, and can be served in myriad ways. Here tomato sauce is combined with Japanese *chawanmushi* (steamed egg custard) to create a dish that looks as good as it tastes. *Yuba* adds textural intrigue, while pickled plums ensure an ingenious balance of tartness and umami.

SERVES 1

Egg mixture

¼ cup (60 ml) beaten egg
About ⅔ cup (145 ml) dashi
⅓ tsp. (1.5 g) salt
1 tsp. mirin
1 tsp. usukuchi soy sauce

Tomato sauce

3 tomatoes
2 medium onions
7 oz. (200 g) tomato purée
Sugar to taste
Salt and pepper to taste
3 Tbsp. olive oil

2 Tbsp. *kumiage yuba*
1 *umeboshi*

To make the tomato sauce, peel the tomato and cut into chunks. Mix until puréed in a food processor. Mince the onion and sauté in a pan in the olive oil. Transfer the puréed tomatoes and tomato purée to the pan, season with salt, pepper, and a little sugar, and simmer until thickened a little. Use 2 Tbsp. per serving.

Place yuba and umeboshi in a serving bowl and pour in the egg mixture. Cover and steam on medium heat for 8 to 10 minutes.

While the custard is hot, pour 2 Tbsp. of warm tomato sauce over the custard and serve with a spoon.

TIRADITO WITH KOMBU-MARINATED FLOUNDER AND SCALLOP

Kombu-jime is a clever culinary technique that not only helps to preserve fish, but makes it even tastier. When sashimi is wrapped in kombu, moisture is absorbed by the kombu, making the fish firmer, and the umami of the kombu is transferred, giving the flesh a different taste from the original sashimi. Here katsuobushi has been added to make "umami-jime" with even greater depth of flavor.

Makes 9 slices each of flounder and scallop

3 oz. (90 g) flounder fillet, sashimi quality
3 fresh scallops, sashimi quality
1 oz. (30 g) dried bonito flakes
1 sheet dried kombu, about 8 in. (20 cm) square
Salt
18 cilantro leaves
½ tsp. *aji rocoto*
1 tsp. Soy Sauce Salt

Yuzu Lemon Sauce

2 tsp. *yuzu* citrus juice
4 tsp. lemon juice

Lightly sprinkle the flounder fillet and scallops with salt and the bonito flakes. Moisten the kombu sheet and sandwich the flounder fillet and scallops between the folded-over kombu. Vacuum-pack and leave for 2 hours.

To make the yuzu lemon sauce, combine yuzu juice and lemon juice and set aside.

Cut the founder fillet into 9 thin slices. Cut the scallops horizontally into three slices to make 9 scallop rounds.

To assemble, arrange the flounder and scallop slices on a serving plate and garnish each with a cilantro leaf and a drop of aji rocoto. Drizzle with the yuzu lemon sauce and sprinkle with the Soy Sauce Salt.

MATSUHISA SLIDER WITH TOFU BUNS

Healthy burgers using paté and seafood, on buns of tofu instead of bread. Packed with vegetables and served with a flavorsome sauce, the Matsuhisa slider is not only good for your waistline, but satisfying too.

SERVES 8

Truffle Mayonnaise (mix in advance)

4 oz. (120 g) mayonnaise
1 Tbsp. plus 1 tsp. honey
2 g truffle
1 tsp. *yuzu* juice
¼ tsp. truffle oil

Tomato Ketchup Mustard (mix in advance)

About 6 oz. (170 g) tomato ketchup
5 g mustard paste

Tofu Buns

12 oz. (360 g) drained firm tofu (you may need 2 blocks of tofu)
2 oz. (60 g) *yamato* yam
2 oz. (60 g) egg whites
⅔ Tbsp. mirin
⅔ Tbsp. *usukuchi* soy sauce

Seafood Patties

8½ oz. (250 g) shrimp
About 9 oz. (280 g) scallops, sashimi quality
7 oz. (200 g) crab meat
2 Tbsp. clarified butter

Sautéed Shiitake

4 Tbsp. mirin
2 tsp. soy sauce
4 shiitake mushrooms
2 Tbsp. butter

Fried Onion

1 onion
Bread flour
Oil for deep-frying

8 leaves of bibb lettuce
2 Tbsp. butter
8 cornichons (soak the cornichons in water to remove some saltiness, then soak in 4% salted water overnight)

To make the tofu buns, purée all the tofu buns ingredients in a food processor, divide into 8 pieces (each about 2 oz./60 g), and place in ring molds, each 3 in. (7 cm) in diameter. Bake in a 400°F (200°C) oven for 14 minutes. Cut in half like a hamburger bun and lightly sear only one side of each half (the side which will be exposed).

To make the seafood patties, coarsely chop the shrimp, scallops and crabmeat in a food processor, place in ring molds, each 3 in. (7 cm) in diameter, and refrigerate for an hour. Sauté the patties in clarified butter.

To cook the shiitake mushrooms, first make a mirin and soy sauce mixture by bringing the mirin and soy sauce to a simmer to evaporate the mirin's alcohol. Halve each shiitake horizontally, sauté in butter, add 2 tsp. of the mirin and soy sauce mixture. Swirl the pan and reduce the liquid to give the mushrooms a glossy sheen.

For the onion, thinly slice, dust with bread flour, deep-fry and drain on paper towels.

To assemble, place a bibb lettuce leaf on 8 half-buns. Top each with a seafood patty, a shiitake mushroom slice, some fried onions, 1 Tbsp. of the truffle mayonnaise, 1 Tbsp. of the tomato ketchup mustard, and the other half-bun. Secure each slider with a skewer. Serve with cornichons.

VEGETABLE "MISO"-MARINATED GRILLED BLACK COD

Vegetable pastes are a staple of all NOBU restaurants. A great way to use vegetable scraps, this paste further flavored with the likes of kombu and chili peppers, makes meat, fish and vegetables taste even better. An added bonus is being able to prepare the main dish of black cod and the accompanying pickles at the same time.

SERVES 1

6 oz. (180 g) filet of black cod
Japanese cucumber
Hinona radish

Vegetable "Miso"

17 oz. (500 g) vegetable scraps, such as tomato seeds, broccoli stems, carrot and daikon radish peels, or green parts of spring onions
1 chili pepper
⅓ halapeño pepper
1 clove garlic
3 pieces *tsume*-kombu
1 oz. (35 g) soy sauce salt
½ oz. (15 g) salt

Aji-amarillo Onion

¼ onion, sliced thin
1 tsp. *aji amarillo*
1 tsp. lemon juice
Salt

Mix all the ingredients of the vegetable "miso" in a food processor to make a paste. Cover the cold fillet with some of the paste in a container, marinate for 40 minutes, and take the fillet out. Cover the cucumber and radish with some of the paste in a different container as well.

Combine all the ingredients of the aji-amarillo onion. Roast the black cod fillet in a 300°F (150°C) oven for about 15 minutes. Take out from the oven, remove any bones, and sear under a salamander or broiler.

Arrange the black cod fillet and the aji-amarillo onion on a dish. Slice the cucumber and radish and use as a garnish.

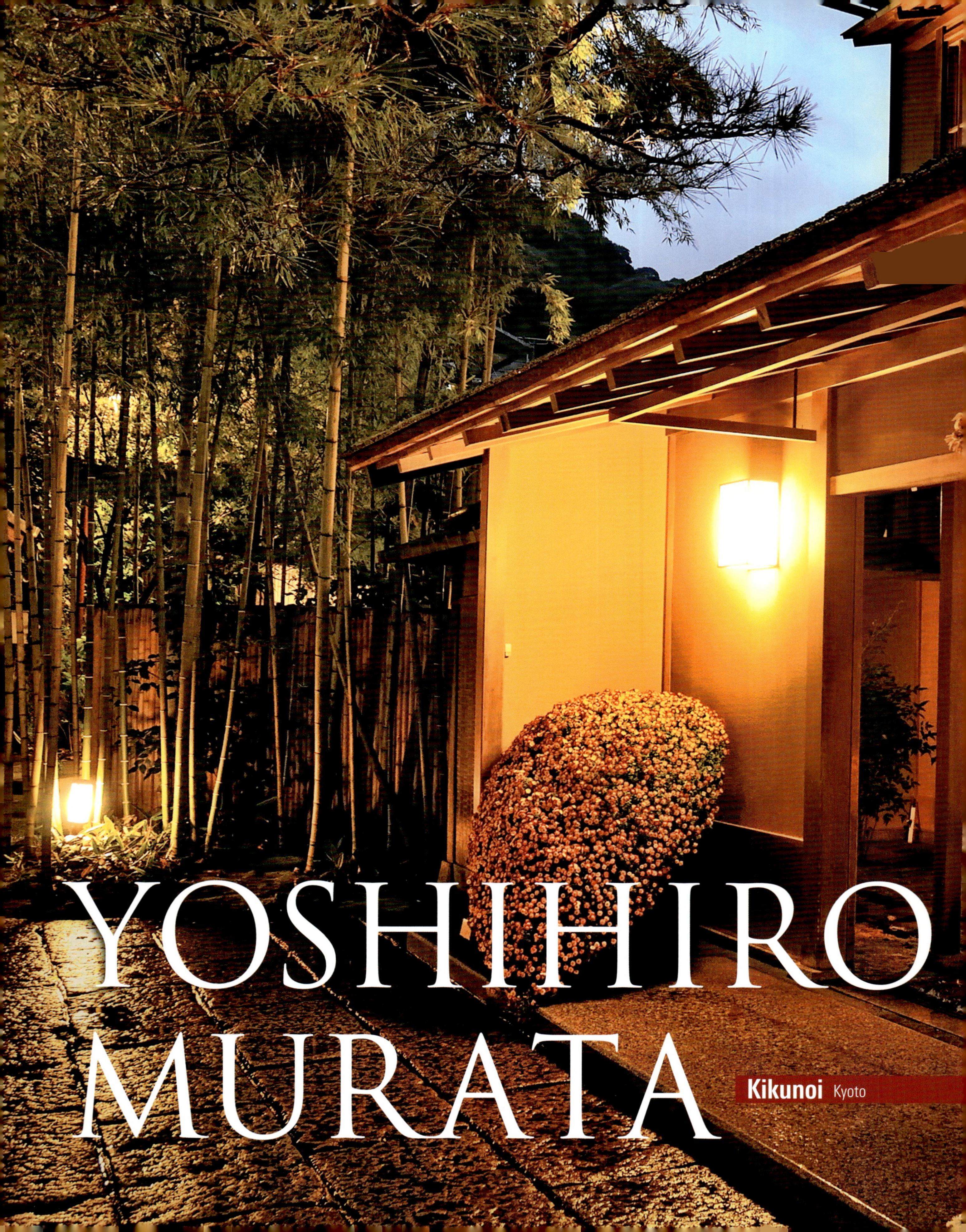

YOSHIHIRO MURATA

Kikunoi Kyoto

At Kikunoi we use ichiban-dashi in all our cooking. Ichiban-dashi makes it easy to adjust the taste for different foods and preparation methods, and it enhances the level of our cuisine, letting us draw out the original flavors of ingredients without overemphasizing the distinctive flavor of the dashi.

Water is also an important element of Japanese cuisine. For many generations my family has preserved a well called *kikusui no i*, literally "chrysanthemum water well," which provided water for use in the tea ceremony. We are now using this water for cooking at Kikunoi. The dashi we make with it has a different taste, and there is also a subtle difference in the flavor of the food we cook with it.

The kombu we use for our dashi is the highest grade product from Kafuka Beach on Rebun Island in Hokkaido, a place well known as a source of high-quality kelp. We age it in a storehouse for a year or more, which gives time for the raw ocean smell to fade, and lets us draw a clear dashi from it. At Kikunoi we strive to draw out a clear umami in all our cooking.

I have many opportunities to cook in other countries, and when I do, I try not to overemphasize the Japanese nature of my cuisine. I just add hints of Japanese taste to the overall fragrance with dashes of Japanese flavorings like *yuzu* (a Japanese citrus fruit) and soy sauce. The ideal is for the food to give off a gentle aroma when served.

I have made it my life's work to promote the spread of Japanese cuisine throughout the world. The best way to do so, I believe, is not to present it too forcefully, but to share the message that Japanese cooking aims for balance.

SIMMERED WINTER VEGETABLES

Cooking vegetables in stock made of the same vegetable comes from the concept of *court-bouillon*. Simmered until tender, ingredients are suffused with dashi for a surprisingly filling all-vegetable dish.

SERVES 4

Turnips

5 small turnips
1¼ cups (300 ml) turnip stock (recipe below)
1¼ cups (300 ml) dashi
4 tsp. *usukuchi* soy sauce
4 tsp. mirin
½ Tbsp. salt

Cut the turnips in half lengthwise and peel off the rind. Combine the turnip stock and dashi in a metal container, cover, and heat in a 212°F (100°C) steamer. Add the turnips, cover, and steam for 20 minutes. Transfer to a saucepan, add the usukuchi soy sauce, mirin and salt, and simmer over low heat for 10 minutes.

Turnip Stock: Combine 8⅔ oz. (250 g) turnip peels, 4⅔ cups (1.2 L) water and ⅙ oz. (5 g) kombu and gently simmer over low heat until reduced by ⅓.

Ebi Taro

2 *ebi* taro
Cloudy, white water leftover from washing rice
4 cups (1 L) dashi
2 Tbsp. *usukuchi* soy sauce
1 oz. plus 1 tsp. (35 g) sugar
2 Tbsp. dried bonito flakes

Peel the ebi taro neatly, making six curved facets on the sides and two flat facets on the top and bottom. Heat the rice-washing water in a metal container in a steamer to 212°F (100°C), add the ebi taro, and cook in the steamer for 20 to 30 minutes. Rinse in cold water, then return to the metal container, add fresh water and place in the steamer again in until tender.

Bring the dashi, usukuchi soy sauce and sugar to a boil in a saucepan. Place the ebi taro in another metal container (or thoroughly drain and wipe the same container) and pour in the hot dashi mixture. Wrap the dried bonito flakes in gauze and place on top. Cover with plastic wrap and cook in a steamer at 185°F (85°C) for 30 minutes.

Carrot

5 pieces carrot, each ½ oz. (15 g)
1¼ cups (300 ml) carrot stock
2 Tbsp. *usukuchi* soy sauce
1 Tbsp. mirin

Peel the carrot and cut into oblique pieces. Simmer in the carrot stock until tender, then add the soy sauce and mirin and simmer for several minutes.

Carrot Stock: Combine 8⅔ oz. (250 g) carrot peel, 5 cups (1.2 L) water and ⅙ oz. (5 g) kombu and gently simmer over low heat until reduced by ⅓.

Turnip leaves

Leaves and stalks from 1 small turnip
About ⅔ cup (180 ml) dashi
1 tsp. *usukuchi* soy sauce
1 g salt

Blanch the turnip leaves, shock in cold water, and drain. Marinate in a mixture of the dashi, usukuchi soy sauce and salt for 3 to 4 hours.

Horikawa Burdock Root

3 pieces *Horikawa* burdock root, each ⅔ oz. (20 g)
Cloudy, white water leftover from washing rice
Scant 1 cup (200 ml) dashi
1 Tbsp. plus 1 tsp. *usukuchi* soy sauce
2 tsp. mirin

Blanch the burdock root pieces in rice-washing water until tender. Rinse in cold water and blanch again in fresh boiling water. Drain well, combine with the dashi, usukuchi soy sauce, and mirin and simmer over low heat for several minutes.

Kujo Onion

4 pieces of *Kujo* onion, each 1½ in. (4 cm) long
⅔ cup plus 4 tsp. (180 ml) dashi
2 tsp. *usukuchi* soy sauce
⅕ tsp. (1 g) salt
1 tsp. mirin

Grill the Kujo onion pieces and marinate in a mixture of the dashi, usukuchi soy sauce, salt, and mirin for 3 to 4 hours.

Chrysanthemum Leaves

½ bunch chrysanthemum leaves
About ⅔ cup (180 ml) dashi
2 tsp. *usukuchi* soy sauce
1 tsp. mirin

Blanch the chrysanthemum leaves, shock in cold water, and squeeze out the excess water. Marinate in a mixture of the dashi, usukuchi soy sauce, and mirin for 3 to 4 hours.

To assemble, arrange all the vegetables in a dish, moisten with about ⅔ cup (150 ml) of the turnip cooking liquid, and garnish with finely sliced yuzu peel.

DUCK DUMPLING SOUP

A covering of very finely sliced turnip resembles thin ice. Underneath, *yomogi mochi* and plum blossom shapes add color to signal the coming of spring.

SERVES 4

1 plus ⅓ *Shogoin* turnip
4 pieces Kujo onion, each 1¼ in. (3 cm) long
4 pieces *yomogi mochi*
2 *kuwai* roots
1 tsp. *kuchinashi* (dried gardenia fruit)
Vegetables cut or punched into flower shapes, such as carrot, *yuzu* peel, and turnip (carrot and turnip should be cooked until tender in the simmering liquid)

Duck Dumplings

3⅓ oz. (100 g) ground duck breast
⅓ oz. (10 g) grated *maru* yam
1⅓ oz. (40 g) raw *surimi*
Powdered sansho pepper
1 tsp. soy sauce

Simmering liquid

2¼ cups (540 ml) dashi
1 Tbsp. *usukuchi* soy sauce
½ tsp. salt

Broth

2½ cups (600 ml) dashi
1 Tbsp. *usukuchi* soy sauce
½ tsp. salt
½ tsp. juice squeezed from grated ginger
1½ Tbsp. *kudzu* slurry (equal parts *kudzu* starch and cold water)

Gold leaf

Peel the whole turnip into a cylinder about 4 in. (10 cm) in diameter and cut the cylinder into 1 mm thick rounds.

Grate the ⅓ turnip and squeeze to make juice. Add a little salt to the juice, heat until the juice becomes translucent, cool, and skim. Add the sliced turnip and heat to 125°F (60°C) for 10 minutes.

Toast the yomogi mochi. Grill the Kujo onion pieces.

Cut the kuwai in half lengthwise and trim into a votive tablet shape. Boil the kuchinashi in water until the water turns a deep orange color. Simmer the kuwai in the water until dyed yellow. Drain and brand a mark on one side of the kuwai with a red hot iron. Cook in the duck simmering liquid for 4 to 5 minutes.

To make the duck dumplings, grind all the ingredients with a mortar and pestle to make a paste. Bring the cooking liquid to a boil in a saucepan. Drop balls of the duck paste into the liquid and simmer until the dumplings are cooked through.

Bring the ingredients of the broth, except the ginger juice and kudzu slurry, to a boil in another saucepan, add the grilled Kujo onion pieces, simmer for 1 to 2 minutes, and take them out. Add about ⅔ cup (150 ml) of the soup that the duck dumplings were cooked in. Adjust the taste with the ginger juice and thicken with the kudzu slurry.

To assemble, place a dumpling, a Kujo onion piece, a piece of grilled yomogi mochi, and a piece of kuwai into each bowl and pour in the thickened broth. Float a slice of turnip on the broth, being careful not to create air pockets, so that the turnip slice resembles a sheet of ice. Garnish with the flower-shaped carrot, turnip, and yuzu peel and a few pieces of gold leaf.

ISE LOBSTER STEAMED IN ITS SHELL

"Gusoku-ni" is the Japanese term for cooking the likes of lobster, prawns and crab in the shell. This dish is similar to bouillabaisse the lobster soup made using oven-roasted shells for a more intense flavor resembling *Sauce Américaine*. To serve, divide onto dishes and pour the juices over top as a sauce.

SERVES 3

Ise Lobster

3 *Ise* lobster halves in the shell, 26 oz. (750 g) total
1¼ cups (300 ml) sake
½ cup (100 ml) *Ise* lobster stock (recipe below)

Broth

Dashi as needed
Additional lobster stock as needed
4 oz. (110 g) white miso
A little soy sauce
2 tsp. juice squeezed from grated ginger

9 snow peas, blanched and marinated in a mixture of about ⅓ cup (90 ml) dashi, ½ tsp. *usukuchi* soy sauce, and a pinch of salt.
Ginger, finely shredded

Lobster Stock: combine 5 oz. (150 g) roasted Ise lobster shells, Scant 4 cups (900 ml) water, 1¼ cups (300 ml) sake and ⅓ oz. (10 g) kombu and gently simmer over low heat until reduced by ⅔.

Clean the Ise lobster halves and tie up the legs, antennae and tails with strips of dried bamboo sheath. Place the lobster in a pan in a single layer, add the sake and stock, cover with a lid, and turn on a heat. Cook, shaking the pan to bring the liquid up over the lobster from time to time, until the flesh of the lobster becomes slightly opaque. Take out the lobster and remove from its shell.

To make the broth, combine the steaming liquid with additional lobster stock and dashi, making 3⅓ cups (800 ml) for 3 servings. Warm the broth and stir in the white miso. Add the lobster shells and simmer for several minutes to bring out more lobster flavor.

Remove the shells and add the lobster meat. Gently warm the lobster meat, take out of the broth, and cut into pieces. Season the soup with a little soy sauce and ginger juice.

To assemble, untie the shells, return the cut lobster meat into each shell, and arrange into serving bowls. Pour in a generous amount of broth and garnish with the snow peas and a mound of shredded ginger.

DUCK BREAST "JIBU-NI"

Dusting the duck with arrowroot powder seals in flavor and thickens the juices. Daikon and duck are simmered in duck dashi made from a combination of roasted duck carcass and kombu dashi. Daikon serves as an excellent foil for the duck's robust flavor.

SERVES 4

Shogoin Daikon Radish

4 cubes of *Shogoin* daikon radish, a little larger than bite sized
Scant 1 cup (200 ml) duck stock (recipe below)
⅔ cup plus 8 tsp. (200 ml) kombu dashi
1 tsp. *usukuchi* soy sauce
½ tsp. mirin
½ tsp. salt

8 pieces duck breast, each ½ oz. (15 g)
Powdered *kudzu* starch
2 *Kujo* green onions
Powdered *sansho* pepper

Cooking liquid

⅔ cup (150 ml) duck stock
⅔ cup (150 ml) kombu dashi
3 Tbsp. plus 1 tsp. soy sauce
3 Tbsp. plus 1 tsp. mirin
1 tsp. sugar

Combine the Shogoin daikon radish, duck stock, and kombu dashi in a metal container, cover, and cook at 212°F (100°C) in a steamer for 20 to 30 minutes until tender. Transfer to a saucepan, add the usukuchi soy sauce, mirin, and salt and gently simmer over low heat for 7 to 8 minutes.

Combine all the ingredients of the cooking liquid in another saucepan and bring to a boil. Dust the duck pieces with the powdered kudzu and briefly cook in the liquid until the duck is just cooked and the kudzu becomes translucent.

To assemble, arrange the duck pieces and Shogoin daikon radish in a dish. Bring the soup to a boil again, add the Kujo onion and simmer for 1 to 2 minutes, then add the onion to the dish along with about ½ cup (150 ml) of the simmering liquid. Sprinkle with powdered sansho pepper.

Duck Stock: Rub 5 oz. (150 g) duck scraps and bones with ½ tsp. salt, leave at least an hour, and roast at 350°F (180°C) for 30 minutes. Combine the roasted duck with about 2½ cups (620 ml) water, about ½ cup (100 ml) sake, a ⅓-oz. (10-g) piece of ginger, a 2-in. (5-cm) long piece of naganegi onion and a ⅔-oz. (20-g) piece of carrot. Gently simmer over low heat until reduced by ⅓. This recipe makes 2 cups (480 ml) duck stock.

Umami synergy: This is how it works

Two to tango

In 1908, the Japanese professor Kikunae Ikeda studied *kombu* and *dashi*, and discovered that glutamate is the key source of the rich taste of *dashi*, in the same way that table salt is the key source of saltiness and household sugar is a key source of sweetness. He concluded that this taste was unique and deserved its own name: *umami*. Moreover, he boldly suggested that umami should join the exclusive rank of basic tastes as a "fifth taste," along with the four then-accepted tastes: salty, sweet, bitter, and sour. However, it would take almost a hundred years before umami became generally accepted as a basic taste.

Along the way toward acceptance of umami as a basic taste lay two other landmark discoveries by Japanese scientists, finally leading to a physiological understanding of the fifth taste. In 1913 Dr. Shintaro Kodama discovered that the other component of Japanese dashi, *katsuobushi*, contained large amounts of a ribonucleotide, inosinate, which also contributes to umami. A third Japanese researcher, Dr. Akira Kuninaka, in 1957 discovered and identified another ribonucleotide, guanylate, that also has umami. Subsequently, the presence of guanylate was detected in dried *shiitake* mushrooms, whose rich umami was already well known to both Japanese and Chinese cooks. Dried shiitake mushrooms were used to replace *katsuobushi* in the classical vegetarian *dashi*, *shōjin dashi*, which is at the very center of the famous Japanese "enlightened kitchen" (*shōjin ryōri*).

More importantly, Dr. Kuninaka undertook further research and found that there is a synergistic interaction between glutamate on one side and inosinate and guanylate on the other. Small quantities of one substance significantly amplify the taste of the other. This was a significant breakthrough in umami research, and highlighted that the real secret behind umami is the combination of basal umami, induced by free glutamate, and synergistic umami induced by free nucleotides: *it takes two to tango.*

Umami becomes a true basic taste

Ikeda's discovery from 1908 was published in a Japanese scientific journal in 1909, but was only translated and published in English in 2002. The publication signaled the full recognition of Ikeda's groundbreaking work and was precipitated by the discovery in 2000 and 2002, by two groups of American scientists, of umami taste receptors in our taste buds. Specific receptor molecules sensitive to glutamate and nucleotides were taken to be the tangible and conclusive scientific evidence for umami being a true basic taste.

This was only the beginning. In recent years scientists from different fields have studied in great detail one of the umami receptors, the so-called T1R1/T1R3

Ole G. Mouritsen
Professor Ph.D. DSc, University of Southern Denmark and Nordic Food Lab

receptor, and the inner workings of this molecule have been revealed. These studies have clarified the mechanism behind the synergy in umami sensation: now we know why it takes two to tango.

Umami sensation works like Pac-Man

The umami receptor has a motif, called a Venus flytrap motif, which looks like a hinge where the binding sites for glutamate and nucleotides reside. Glutamate can bind at the inner wedge of the hinge and the nucleotides at the edges. Upon binding, a signal is sent to the taste center of the brain, which says: umami! The binding of glutamate is strongly enhanced if a nucleotide binds at the same time.

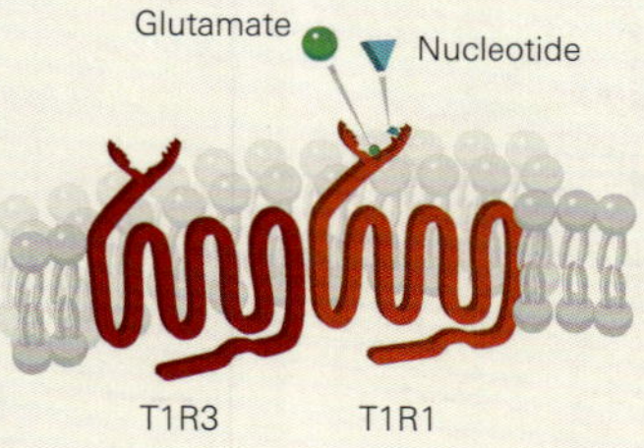

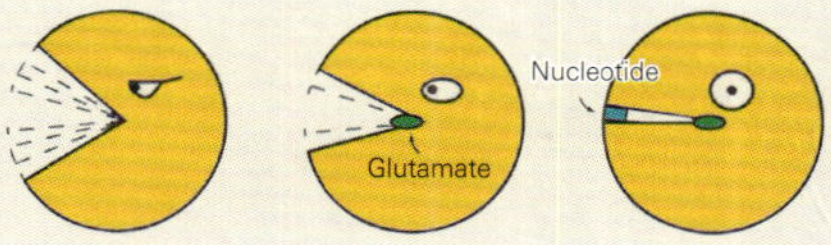

LEFT: Schematic illustration of the T1R1/T1R3 umami receptor highlighting the binding motif exposing the binding sites of basal umami (glutamate) and synergistic umami (nucleotide). RIGHT: Cartoon illustration of the synergistic mechanism demonstrating, by a Pac-Man analogy, the enhanced binding of glutamate upon co-binding of a nucleotide.

The molecular mechanism behind this enhanced binding resembles the action of Pac-Man. In the absence of both glutamate and nucleotides, the snapping of the jaws of Pac-Man is very fast and there is no umami sensation. Upon the binding of glutamate in his throat, the snapping motion of Pac-Man is dampened and umami sensation occurs. However, upon simultaneous binding of nucleotides at his lips, the jaws snaps shut, glutamate becomes more strongly bound, and the full sensation of umami synergy sets in.

Umami synergy around the world

The synergy in umami sensation is a true pairing principle based on solid science and is a universal trait, in contrast to the traditional pairing hypothesis for different types of foodstuffs, which has been shown to be dependent on food culture and adaptation. Cuisines around the world use universal umami synergy and pairing of glutamate and nucleotides in many traditional and innovative dishes. There are a few raw ingredients that can provide umami synergy on their own (sun-ripened tomatoes and *nori* used for sushi are two prominent examples).

Basal umami: glutamate	Synergistic umami: nucleotides
Kombu	*Katsuobushi/Shiitake*
Eggs	Bacon
Cheese	Ham
Tomatoes	Beef
Vegetables	Meat
Green peas	Scallops

Well-known pairing for optimal umami synergy

LITERATURE

O.G. Mouritsen & K. Styrbæk, *Umami: Uncovering the Secrets of the Fifth Taste* (New York: Columbia University Press, 2014).

O.G. Mouritsen & H. Khandelia, "Molecular mechanism of the allosteric enhancement of the umami taste sensation," *FEBS Journal* 279 (2012): 3112-20.

DESSE

REGIS CURSAN **NOBU** London

RTS

KEIKO NAGAE Paris

REGIS CURSAN

Hinode

The first time I ate tamarillo I could feel something was different from other fruits. Once it was certified by the Umami Information Center, I could say that the reaction I had was umami-related. While playing with different combinations, I thought about regrouping those flavors to create a new dessert.

Maybe I was the first one to discover umami in the tamarillo!

Strawberry Kanten

Makes about 6

500 g (16⅔ oz.) frozen strawberry
50 g (1⅔ oz.) sucrose
3 g kanten

Mix the frozen strawberry with the sugar, then heat in a microwave for 9 minutes.

Sieve gently without crushing the fruit to obtain about 9 oz. (260 g) of "nectar."

Take the "nectar," add kanten and boil for 30 seconds.

Remove the kanten mix from the heat, strain through a fine sieve, and cool in a metal container.

Use 1⅔ oz. (50 g) for the "sun" (3 in./80 mm diameter) and ⅓ oz. (10 g) for the cheese cake tops.

Oat Cookie

Makes about 140

690 g (23 oz.) French butter
600 g (20 oz.) Demerara sugar
810 g (27 oz.) flour
18 g baking powder
9 g salt
150 g (5 oz.) organic oats
60 g (2 oz.) oats
Additional butter for the crumble

Let butter warm to room temperature.

Mix flour with the baking powder, salt, organic oats, and grained oats.

Put butter and sugar in a mixer with a paddle attachment and start to turn. Add the flour mixture in several additions.

Take the dough out onto a baking sheet and keep in the fridge to set. Shape and cut some of the dough for cookies to go under the sorbet.

Grate the remaining dough and store in the fridge.

Bake the grated dough and the cookies at 330°F (165°C), ½ fan, until they turn golden.

Make crumble powder in a blender from the baked grated dough and soft butter (20% of the grated cookie by weight). Roll out ⅛ in. (3 mm) thick and cut out with a 2 in. (4.5 cm) ring mold for the cheese cake bases. Store on a baking tray with ring molds still around the cheese cake bases.

Cheese Cake

Makes about 26

450 g (15 oz.) cream cheese
200 g (7 oz.) sucrose
½ pod Madagascar vanilla
100 g (3½ oz.) whole eggs pasteurized
30 g milk
560 g (18⅔ oz.) crème fraîche

2.5 g custard stabilizer

Weigh all the liquid in a bowl. Mix well, then add all the dry ingredients and mix to obtain a smooth texture. Store in the fridge in piping bags.

Pipe 1⅔ oz. (50 g) into each prepared ring (see "Oat Cookie" above) and cook for 20 minutes at 230°F (110°C) with ½ fan.

Cool down and finish with strawberry kanten on top. Store in a fridge.

Tamarillo Sorbet

Makes about 30 portions

400 g (14 oz.) fresh tamarillo purée
350 g (350 ml) water
150 g (5 oz.) dextrose
93 g sucrose
4 g stabilizer

Combine water, dextrose, sucrose, and stabilizer (and heat to 185°F/85°C) to make a syrup.

Cool it down until it drops below 4°C (39°F) and mix with the tamarillo purée using a hand blender. Store for 24 hours in the fridge.

On the next day churn and store in the freezer.

Assembly

Black sesame paste

Place a strawberry kanten "sun" in the center of each plate. Cut out a bit at the top with a 2 in. (4.5 cm) ring mold and place a cheese cake in the cut-out. Draw a line of black sesame paste with a brush. Place an oat cookie on the plate and top it with the sorbet.

Kurama

The cut of the chocolate decoration was inspired by the legend from Mount Kurama where a Buddhist monk (an expert in the art of the sword) was suddenly attacked by a giant snake. His skills prevailed, and he cut the giant snake in two, killing it.

This eclectic combination of chocolate and tamarillo, sesame and yuzu, creates in an intriguing balance of East and West.

Sesame Crunch

Makes about 120
50 g (1⅔ oz.) praline
100 g (3½ oz.) milk chocolate
70 g (2⅓ oz.) sesame nougat powder

Melt chocolate and add praline and nougat powder.

Spread the mixture onto round chablons on a baking sheet and set in the freezer Once frozen, collect and store the sesame crunch discs.

Dulce de Leche Ice cream

Makes about 35
532 g milk
266 g (9 oz.) whipping cream (32% milkfat)
32 g (1 oz.) glucose syrup
21 g (⅔ oz.) inverted sugar
37 g (1⅓ oz.) skim milk powder
106 g (3⅓ oz.) sucrose
4 g stabilizer (Leagel Neutro Latte 5)
30 g (1 oz.) dulce de leche

Warm up milk, cream, glucose, and inverted sugar in a pot and bring to 105°F (40°C).

Add milk powder and mix until it disolves.

Add sucrose and stabilizer and cook to 185°F (85°C).

Sieve it and cool it down until it drops below 40°F (4°C).

Add the dulce de leche and mix with a hand blender.

Store for 24 hours in the fridge, churn the next day, and store in the freezer.

Yuzu Syrup

50 g *yuzu* juice
100 g (100 ml) water
30 g (1 oz.) sucrose

Combine water and sugar in a pot and bring to a boil to make syrup. Cool it down and add yuzu juice.

Lemon and Yuzu Sponge Cake

Makes about 20
150 g (5 oz.) pasteurized whole egg
275 g (9 oz.) sucrose
188 g milk
62 g (2 oz.) almonds
250 g (8 oz.) flour
10 g (⅓ oz.) baking powder
2 g lemon zest
150 g olive oil

Infuse the olive oil with lemon zest Put almonds, flour, and baking powder in a blender and mix. Whip eggs and sugar until it forms peaks.

Mix the milk into the egg. Fold in the flour, then the infused oil.

Spread on a baking sheet and bake at 375°F (190°C) for 7 minutes. Using a brush, soak the sponge cake with generous amount of yuzu syrup.

Tamarillo and Milk chocolate Mousse

950 g (33 oz.) tamarillo purée
1.3 kg (2.8 lbs.) milk chocolate
8 g gelatin leaves
1.1 kg (2.4 lbs.) whipping cream (32% milkfat)
Chocolate for spraying

Line 2⅓ in. (6 cm) ring molds with acetate paper and place on a sheet tray with acetate paper on top of Silpat

Melt chocolate and keep it at 105°F (40°C).

Soak the gelatin in cold water. Warm up a bit of the purée and add the gelatin. Then add the rest of the purée. Pour the purée into chocolate and make ganache.

Whip the cream to soft peaks.

Add a little cream to the ganache at 100°F (38°C), then add the rest of the cream.

Pipe the mousse into the ring molds up to half way. Put the sesame crunch disc in each ring, then fill the rings with more mousse and top with sponge cake cut into rounds.

Set in the freezer, unmold, and paint them black with chocolate spray the next day.

Assembly

NOBU Miso salt
Yuzu jelly
Chocolate tube, cut on a bias

Defrost mousse in fridge 1 hour before serving.

Spread dulce de leche on each plate using a template. Sprinkle Nobu miso salt on the dulce de leche. Place a chocolate tube at the top of the dulce de leche. Place the mousse on the plate and the ice cream on top of a rectangular piece of sponge cake. Garnish the mousse with a dot of yuzu jelly.

REGIS CURSAN

KEIKO NAGAE

TROPICAL FRUITS AND PARMIGIANO-REGGIANO CREAM

While each ingredient here has its own distinct character, none dominates: thus balance is maintained. Tastes change as you eat, with umami lingering afterward.

Makes 15 servings

Parmigiano Cream

200 g (200 ml) milk
200 g (200 ml) fresh cream (35% fat)
70 g (2⅓ oz.) aged Parmigiano-Reggiano cheese (adjust quantity depending its age and quality)
100 g (3½ oz.) egg yolks

Mix the egg yolks and granulated sugar in a bowl. Heat the milk, fresh cream and cheese in a saucepan until warm. Slowly mix half the heated milk mixture into the bowl of egg-sugar mixture, then return the entire contents of the bowl to the saucepan. Continue to heat, keeping it at 180 to 182°F (82 to 83°C) and stirring constantly, until the mixture becomes thickened.

Transfer the mixture to a bowl and cool rapidly.

Fill an espuma canister with the ¾ of the Parmigiano cream. Follow the instructions for preparing the espuma.

Refrigerate the remaining Parmigiano cream.

Passion Fruit Gelée

100 g (100 ml) apple juice
100 g (3½ oz.) passion fruit purée
30 g granulated sugar
2.5 g pectin NH (Louis François)
100 g (3½ oz.) passion fruit seeds

Heat the apple juice and passion fruit purée in a saucepan to 105°F (40°C), then add the sugar and pectin mixture by sprinkling it through a sieve. Bring to a boil and skim. Add the passion fruit seeds, bring to a boil again, and skim. Remove from the heat and cool.

Candied Pineapple

20 g brown sugar
7 oz. (200 g) ripe Victorian pineapple, cut into ½-in. (1-cm) cubes
Vanilla seeds from ¼ Tahitian vanilla bean

Melt the brown sugar in a frying pan, add the pineapple pieces and vanilla beans and sauté. The pineapple pieces will release their juice. Continue to sauté until the pineapple becomes translucent. Remove from the heat and allow to rest.

Pineapple Sorbet

Makes 20 portions
35 g (1 oz.) granulated sugar
15 g powdered glucose
500 g (17 oz.) Victorian pineapple purée
100 g (100 ml) water

In a sauce pan, bring the granulated sugar and powdered glucose to a boil to make a syrup. Cool, combine with the pineapple purée, transfer to a Pacojet canister to cool to room temperature. Freeze.
*When using fully ripe pineapple, just purée and freeze a Pacojet canister.

Pineapple Chips

½ pineapple

Slice the pineapple into 1 mm thick half-rounds and dry in a food dryer.

Coconut Tuiles

Makes 12 to 15
50 g (1⅔ oz.) dried coconut
50 g (1⅔ oz.) granulated sugar
25 g (About 1 oz.) unsalted butter
50 g (1⅔ oz.) egg whites

Mix the dried coconut, granulated sugar, and butter in a food processor. Add the egg whites, mix, and allow to rest in a refrigerator.

Spread the mixture on a silicone baking mat in circles 1¼ in. (3 cm) in diameter and bake at 300°F (150°C) for 10 to 12 minutes.

Assembly

1 Tbsp. minced ginger
Cilantro flowers

Run the frozen pineapple purée canisters through the Pacojet to make sorbet. Spoon the Parmigiano cream into serving dishes. Mix the sautéed pineapple and ginger and place on the cream. Top each with the passion fruit gelée, a coconut tuile, Parmigiano cream espuma, and a quenelle of pineapple sorbet. Garnish with a pineapple chip and cilantro flowers.

CRISPY MATCHA PARFAIT, RASPBERRIES, AND GREEN TEA UMAMI GELÉE

Tea is high in umami. The sparing use of sugar in this dessert featuring all five basic tastes is amply compensated for by the satisfaction of umami.

Makes 10 servings

Crispy Matcha Mousse

Matcha Parfait

About 75 g (2⅔ oz.) egg yolks
60 g (2 oz.) granulated sugar
95 g milk
10 g (⅓ oz.). *matcha*
210 g (7 oz.) whipping cream

White Chocolate Glaze

150 g (5 oz.) white chocolate, chopped
50 g (1⅔ oz.) cocoa butter
Toasted brown rice

To make the matcha mousse, add some of the milk to the matcha, dissolve, and mix with rest of the milk. Mix the egg yolks and granulated sugar well and combine with the matcha milk. Heat in a water bath, keeping it at 180°F (82°C) and stirring continuously, until thickened.

Whip the mixture in a mixer until it cools to room temperature and combine with freshly whipped cream. Pour into a tray 1 in. (2.5 cm) deep, flatten the surface and freeze. Cut into discs 1¾ in. (4 cm) in diameter and keep frozen.

To make the white chocolate glaze, melt the white chocolate and cocoa butter in a bowl in a hot water bath, controlling the temperature to keep it below 105°F (40°C). Skewer each frozen mousse disc with a toothpick and coat the bottom and sides with the white chocolate glaze. Roll in the toasted brown rice.

Matcha Sponge Cake

5 oz. (150 g) egg whites
25 g (About 1 oz.) granulated sugar
25 g (About 1 oz.) almond flour
10 g (⅓ oz.) unsalted butter
10 g (⅓ oz.) flour
10 g (⅓ oz.) *matcha*

Mix all the ingredients in a Thermomix. Fill an espuma canister and follow the instructions for preparing the espuma.

Use plastic cups that are 1 in. (2.5 cm) high and more than 1¾ in. (4 cm) in diameter. Poke several holes on the cups, foam in about ½ oz. (14 g) of the espuma and microwave at 600 or 700 Watts for about 35 seconds.

Remove the cakes from the cups, cut into cylinders using a 1¾ in. (4 cm) ring mold and trim the cylinders to 1 in (2.5 cm) high.

Raspberry Compote

100 g (3½ oz.) raspberry purée
40 g (1⅓ oz.) granulated sugar
60 g (2 oz.) frozen or fresh broken raspberries
2.4 g of 200-bloom gelatin

Heat the raspberry purée until warm. Add the granulated sugar and broken raspberries and heat but do not boil. Mix in the gelatin and remove from the heat. Pour into 1¾ in. (4 cm) round silicone molds until the mixture reaches ¼ in. (5 mm) high. Freeze.

Spun Sugar

100 g (3⅓ oz.) granulated sugar
50 g (50 ml) water
25 g glucose
12 g *Nougasec*

Combine all the ingredients in a saucepan and reduce to 338°F (170°C). Make the spun sugar and keep dry.

Sencha Umami Gelée

200 g (200 ml) soft water
10 g (⅓ oz.) *sencha* green tea leaves
0.4 g xanthan gum

Bring the soft water to a boil, cool to about 70°F (22°C), brew the tea for 5 minutes and strain well. Add the xanthan gum into the tea and mix with a stick blender. Compress in a vacuum pack to remove air.

Assembling

Fresh raspberries, halved if large
Gold leaf

Stack a frozen raspberry compote disc on each crispy matcha mousse disc and leave at room temperature for 5 minutes.

Spoon some sencha umami gelée on each plate and place a mousse and raspberry compote stack on the gelée. Layer on a disc of warm matcha sponge cake and top with the fresh raspberries. Garnish with spun sugar and gold leaf.

A PRACTICAL GUIDE TO DASHI AND UMAMI

Making dashi

It would be fair to say that the flavor of a Japanese dish is determined by the quality of its dashi. Here are the basic methods for three of the most popular kinds of dashi.

ICHIBAN DASHI

Ichiban (primary) dashi is the closest thing to pure umami broth. Made from the finest possible ingredients, it is untinged with the bitterness that often comes from making dashi with other ingredients. It draws out the flavor of other foods without calling too much attention to itself. Its clarity and subtle aroma make ichiban dashi ideal for soup.

1.8 L soft water
1 oz. (30 g) *Rishiri* kombu (dried kelp harvested near Rishiri, Hokkaido)
1⅔ oz. (50 g) shaved *honkarebushi* (dried bonito flakes), *chiai* (blood line) removed

1 Combine the water and the kombu in a pan over very low heat.

2 Slowly heat the pan until the water reaches 140°F (60°C), and hold the water at that temperature for 1 hour to extract the maximum umami from the kombu.

3 Remove the kombu and raise the temperature of the water to 185°F (85°C). Turn off the heat and add the bonito flakes.

4 When the bonito flakes have thoroughly hydrated, leave about 10 more seconds, then strain through a fine sieve covered with cheese cloth. Never squeeze the bonito flakes, but let the liquid drain naturally.

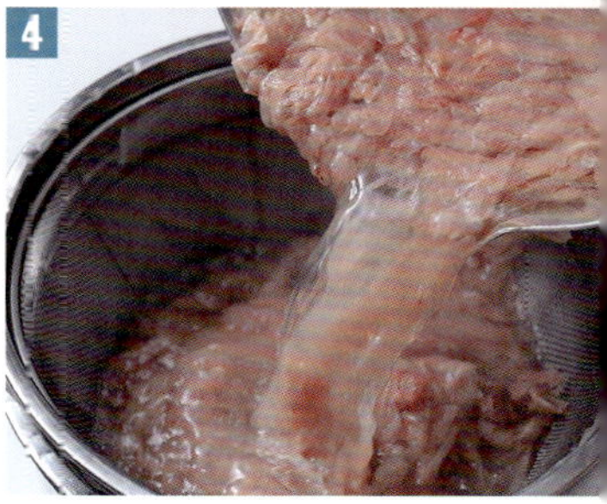

RECIPE BY KIKUNOI

KOMBU DASHI

Dashi made solely from kombu is mild and subtle, perfect for delicately-flavored dishes that capitalize on the taste and aroma of their other ingredients.

1.8 L soft water
1 oz. (30 g) *Rishiri* kombu

1 Combine the water and the kombu in a pan over very low heat.

2 Slowly heat the water to 140°F (60°C) and hold at that temperature for 1 hour to extract the maximum umami from the kombu. Remove the kombu.

RECIPE BY KIKUNOI

SHIITAKE MUSHROOM DASHI

Dashi made from dried shiitake mushrooms is a kind of *shojin* or vegetarian dashi, offering intense aroma and umami.

1.8 L soft water
1⅔ oz. (50 g) dried shiitake mushroom

1 Wash any dirt or other impurities off the shiitake mushrooms without letting them soak. Place them in a bowl with the water and leave to soak overnight.

2 Strain through a fine sieve covered with cheese cloth.

RECIPE BY KIKUNOI

Dashi and umami

Basic information and ways to learn more

Kumiko Ninomiya, Ph.D. Umami Information Center
Yukiyo Katsuta Umami Information Center

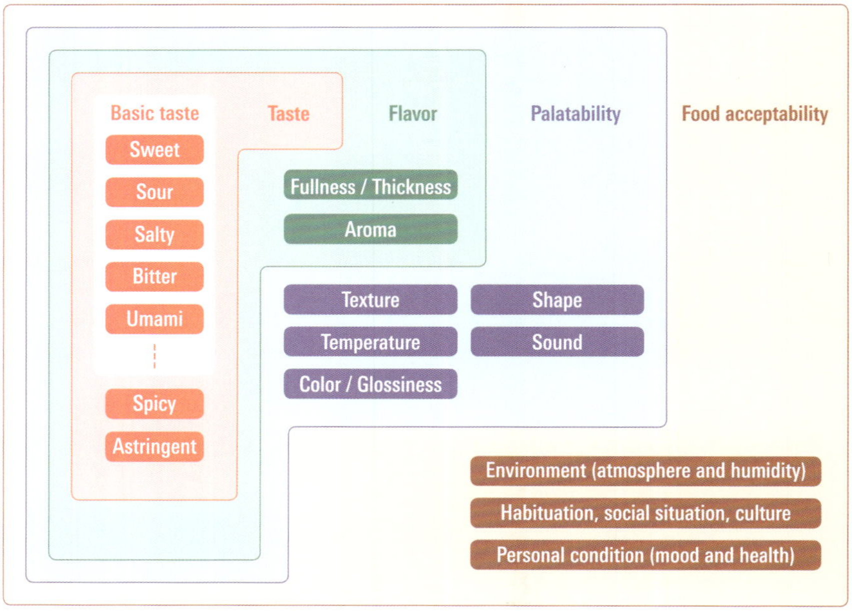

How humans experience their food

Umami basics

What is umami?

Umami is the taste imparted by a number of substances, predominantly the amino acid *glutamate* and 5'-ribonucleotides such as *inosinate* and *guanylate*. Umami is a subtle taste, usually overshadowed by other tastes. We may not recognize it if someone else does not point out its presence. Although umami itself is not an outstanding taste, it becomes indispensable for harmonizing with the other basic tastes and bringing out the characteristic taste of many foods.

The chefs featured in this book describe umami in many ways: a delicate taste, a mild, subtle taste, a taste that spreads across the tongue, enveloping it completely, lasting longer than other tastes, a mouth-watering sensation. Those of you that are just starting to understand umami and incorporate umami in your cooking may find it difficult to imagine just how umami tastes from these comments. But once you become acquainted with the taste, you will enjoy the challenge of combining umami-rich foods and extracting umami to make original broths and stocks. Umami not only helps us to create more flavorful dishes, but also to serve healthier foods with less salt or animal fat. We hope that by reading this book, you will understand the unique characteristics of umami, and by actually tasting umami through your own experiments, you will learn to use umami ingredients with more confidence.

Deliciousness and umami

Since the word "umami" is originally Japanese and the expressions "to have umami" and "umai" can mean "tastiness" or "deliciousness," "umami" is often confused with "deliciousness." Whether something tastes good or not is a comprehensive, yet subjective evaluation determined by elements such as taste, aroma, texture and temperature, besides other factors such as appearance, color and shape, as well as one's physical condition, surrounding environment, cultural background, and previous experiences. Of these various elements, umami in balance with the other basic tastes (sweet, sour, salty, and bitter) plays an important role in determining the deliciousness of a dish.

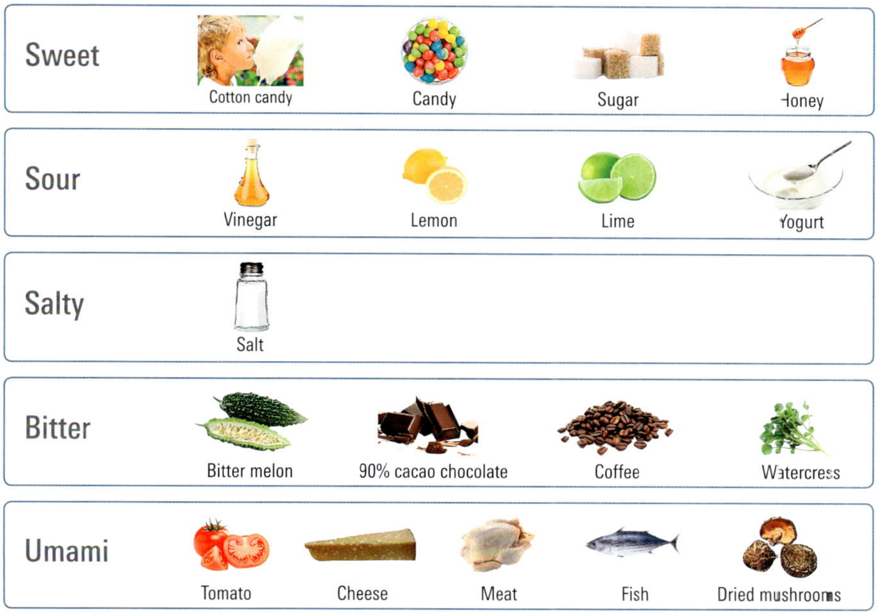

Five basic tastes and related food

Professor Kikunae Ikeda

What are the basic tastes?

The taste of a grapefruit, to take one example, is composed of sourness, bitterness and sweetness. Sour, bitter and sweet cannot be broken down into smaller constituent parts or expressed in any other way. The basic tastes are pure, unique tastes that cannot be produced by mixing other tastes. For humans, the ability to detect the basic tastes is essential to survival. The idea that taste is not just a source of enjoyment, but is a set of signals that direct us to satisfy the body's needs or to protect the body from harmful substances, is generally accepted based on physiological and nutritional studies. Sweet is a signal of energy intake from sugar. Sour is a sign of organic acids in unripe fruit and rotting foods. The bitterness of alkaloids enables us to avoid harmful substances, and the saltiness of minerals is necessary to maintain the tonic balance of body fluids. Recent studies suggest that umami signals to the body that we have ingested protein. Umami facilitates the digestion of protein by promoting the secretion of saliva and digestive juices.

Discovery of umami

We can all easily imagine and describe the four basic tastes other than umami—sweet, sour, salty and bitter—because these tastes have clearly defined characteristics, and foods that exhibit each (such as sugar for sweetness or salt for saltiness) have been apparent since ancient times. Moreover, theorists from the philosopher Aristotle, who lived over 2000 years ago, to the early 20th century psychologist Hans Henning, have espoused numerous ideas on the basic tastes other than umami. Umami, however, was only identified a hundred years ago, by Professor Kikunae Ikeda, a Japanese scientist from Kyoto (also, coincidentally, the birthplace of modern Japanese gastronomy).

Ikeda was interested in learning the exact nature of that taste essential to the traditional Japanese soup stock *dashi*—a taste neither sweet, sour, salty nor bitter, yet distinctive—and began studying the dried seaweed *kombu,* which is one of the ingredients used to make dashi.

Monosodium glutamate extracted by Prof. Ikeda

Ikeda discovered that the main component in kombu's distinctive taste was the amino acid glutamate. He continued his research, developing a new seasoning based on glutamate that dissolves easily in water, imparts a powerful umami taste, and does not absorb moisture: MSG (monosodium glutamate).

Other umami substances include nucleotides such as inosinate and guanylate, also discovered by Japanese scientists. Another umami substance inosinate in dried bonito flakes (*katsuobushi*) was discovered by Shintaro Kodama in 1913, and

Umami substances in food ingredients

© Hikari

Akira Kuninaka discovered in 1960 that guanylate also has umami taste and is highly concentrated in dried mushrooms. All these umami substances were discovered in the materials used for making dashi.

Properties of umami

A taste that spreads across the tongue

It has been said that umami is a taste that spreads across the tongue, enveloping the whole of the tongue. Taste maps of the tongue showing which parts are sensitive to different kinds of basic tastes had been used for decades, up until the end of the 1990's. They were a result of the filter paper method, which used small pieces of filter paper with each of the basic tastes placed on different parts of the tongue. The subject's tongue was not moving in this method. At that time, the tip, sides and base of the tongue were found to be variably sensitive to sweet, salty, sour and bitter. However the outcome is different when subjects are asked to lick a small volume of a test solution placed on a spoon and indicate which part of the tongue they perceive its taste. In this more natural tasting paradigm, subjects sensed all tastes over a much wider area of the tongue. It was also confirmed by this study that umami was perceived across a wider area of the tongue than the other four basic tastes, with the base of the tongue particularly receptive. In other words, compared to other tastes, umami is perceived as coating the whole of the tongue.

Lasts longer than other basic tastes

Umami also has a unique characteristic that lingers on the palate. A study has been carried out to investigate the duration of taste, in which solutions displaying salty, sour and umami tastes are sampled. Changes over time in the intensity of taste perceived in the mouth were then investigated. Sour and salty tastes were found to be strongest immediately after being taken into the mouth, before rapidly declining. On the other hand, umami retained its intensity for an extended period. This is why umami provides a subtle aftertaste (in a positive sense), the lingering taste after consuming umami-rich foods.

A mouth-watering sensation

Some chefs have also described umami as a mouth-watering sensation. Research on the physiology of taste has confirmed that the umami substance glutamate does actually promote salivation, and that this secretion of saliva is further encouraged by the presence of inosinate. Everyone has found themselves salivating more when eating a sour food such as lemon, and in fact umami is also known to trigger the secretion of saliva for extended periods.

Without saliva, not only can we not perceive the taste of foods, we cannot swallow them. Saliva also plays a vital role in oral hygiene. Taste impairment among the elderly is often due to a decline in salivation. With some reports suggesting that an impaired sense of taste can be ameliorated using umami to promote salivation, efforts are underway to deploy umami as a way of improving quality of life among the elderly.

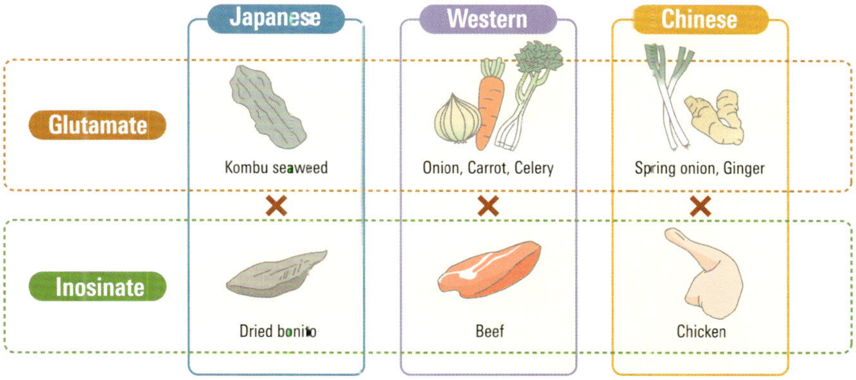

Synergistic effect in various cooking

Effect of umami on the taste of foods

Makes sour and bitter tastes milder

Umami has the effect of moderating sourness and bitterness. Ingredients such as vinegar and the juice of citrus fruits have been widely used since ancient times to impart a fresh tang to cooking. The sourness of these foods comes from organic acids such as acetic and citric acid. Umami ameliorates these sour components with a buffering effect that takes the edge off their tartness. Bitterness is also an important taste that adds a special accent to cooking, but excessive bitterness tends to become acrid. Umami has the effect of masking this quality.

Accentuating each other, umami and salt

Umami is recognized as amplifying saltiness where the salt concentration is less than 1%. Synergy between umami substances has also been found to be highest at this level of salinity (see "Umami synergism" below). Considering that soup ordinarily has a salt concentration of 0.8 to 0.9%, soups could be said to have just the right amount of salt to accentuate umami.

At the same time, it is well documented that umami amplifies saltiness, again, if salt is lower than 1%. When comparing two variations of potato soup containing umami, one at a salt concentration of 0.3% with MSG and the other at 0.5% without MSG, there was no apparent difference in their palatability. If umami is present, a sufficient level of palatability can be maintained even with low salt. MSG contains only 1/3 the amount of sodium as salt (NaCl) and is used at levels far less than salt. Based on these two factors, MSG contributes about 1/20 to 1/30 the amount of sodium as salt.

These effects are not caused by any change in the volume of umami or salt due to the presence of the other. The presence of salt highlights the umami contained in the food, and the presence of umami ensures a feeling of satisfaction even when salt is reduced. Thus the tastes of each are accentuated, and tastiness preserved. The balance between salt and umami is the key to appetizing food. By making clever use of umami in cooking, even those reducing their salt intake for health reasons will find meals containing less salt satisfying.

Umami synergism

When the umami substance glutamate coexists with the nucleotides inosinate, or guanylate, there is a boost in the intensity of the umami above that exhibited by a single umami substance in isolation. This is known as the synergistic effect of umami. Particularly noteworthy is the fact that umami synergy is most intense at a 1:1 ratio of glutamate and inosinate, approximately seven to eight times stronger than when the two are sampled separately. This does not mean that mixing glutamate and inosinate results in an increase in the actual volume of umami substance, but that people can perceive a greater intensity of umami.

Mankind has been making use of umami's synergistic effect since long before this phenomenon was scientifically proved, experientially preparing food in ways that intensify umami, such as making soups combining vegetables high in glutamate with meat high in inosinate, and preparing dashi from glutamate-rich kombu with inosinate-rich bonito flakes.

What is dashi?

Authentic Japanese dashi

Dashi is a fundamental, indispensable component of Japanese cuisine, but unlike the stock or broth of western cuisines, or Chinese broth (*tang*), it is very simple in terms of both ingredients and preparation.

Kombu dashi is one of the most common dashi options, can be prepared by adding a piece of dried kombu seaweed (usually about 6 to 8 in./15 to 20 cm wide and 8 in./20 cm long; which makes a 1 to 2% volume per weight of water) in a pan with a liter of water, and simmering for about an hour on a medium to low heat. The water should not boil. When the cooking is finished, remove the kombu from water. Care must be taken in the preparation of kombu dashi: cooking over too high a heat, or for too long, leaves it bitter and/or slimy.

The main component in kombu dashi prepared in this manner is glutamate, and the dashi's taste could be described as almost pure umami. *Katsuo dashi* made from dried bonito flakes (*katsuobushi*), dashi from dried shiitake mushrooms and *ichiban dashi* combining kombu and bonito flakes are also extraordinarily simple in taste, containing mostly the umami substances glutamate, inosinate, and guanylate.

Ichiban-dashi may also be high in the amino acid histidine from the bonito flakes, which is slightly sour, but doesn't have the same taste impact as glutamate.

Umami: a universal taste

Umami is often mistakenly considered a taste unique to Japanese or other Asian cuisines. It is true that most umami substances were first identified by Japanese scientists. Chinese cuisine generously uses seasonings and condiments high in umami. Other Asian cuisines with their umami-rich fish sauces and pastes have no doubt encouraged the idea of umami as a taste peculiar to Asia. But umami is not unique to Japan, or to the Asian region in general. The broths and stocks of western cooking, and the sauces used in French cooking, capitalize on umami to the greatest possible extent, and umami has been imparting its unique allure to countless dishes for thousands of years. So why does this misconception arise?

There are two reasons. The first is that the oils and animal fats commonly used in western cooking are hardly employed at all in traditional Japanese cuisine: perhaps the absence of oil or fat allowed Japanese people to perceive and appreciate umami that much more intensely. The second is that the dashi of Japan is so simple it could be described as umami itself. Though sugar, a symbol of sweetness, and salt, the archetypal salty taste, did exist in the west, there were no ingredients or foods tasting purely and solely of umami. For instance, *fond* in French cooking is made by simmering meat or bones with aromatic vegetables to make a reduction. Those meat and vegetables include amino acids other than umami substances, which makes for a complex taste.

The fact is, every world cuisine has the same goal (even if its practitioners don't have a word for it): drawing out umami efficiently to make food appetizing. Western cuisine relies on a long cooking process for the extraction and concentration of taste substances from food ingredients such as beef, pork and poultry. As a result, umami harmonizes with the overall flavor. In Japan, food ingredients high in umami are dried slowly over a long period of time to remove moisture, thus concentrating umami in advance. Because of the long drying process, umami can be rapidly extracted during cooking. Neither approach is superior to the other; both are simply different ways of achieving the same goal.

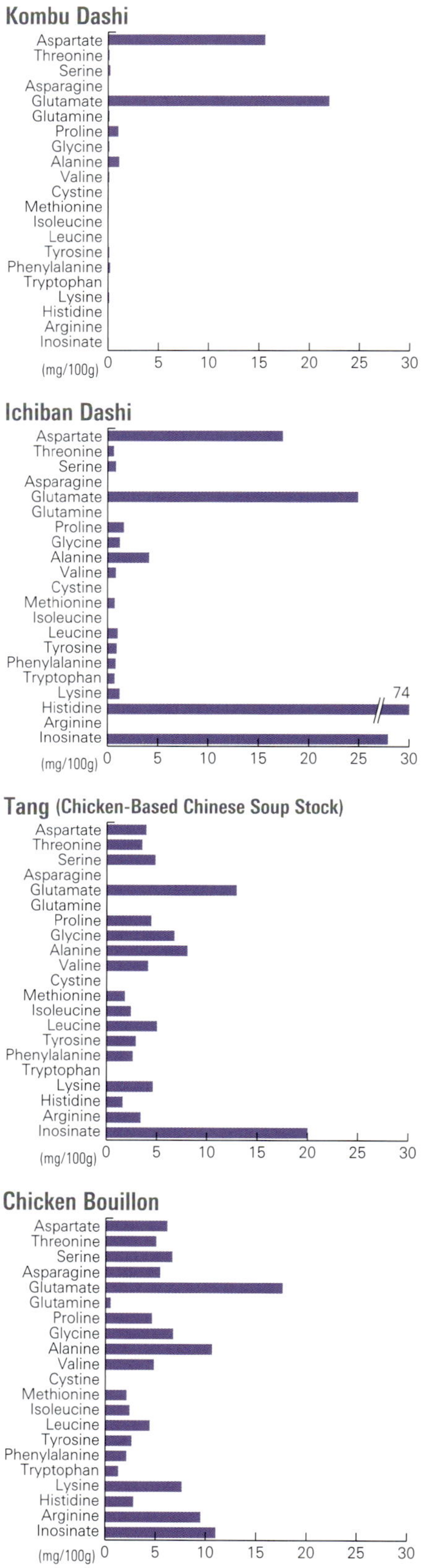

Free amino acid and inosinate composition of various cooking stocks

New style dashi

Yoshihiro Murata

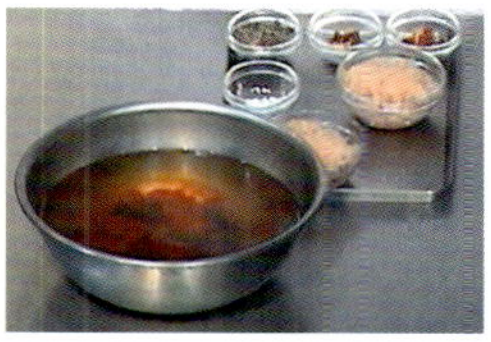

INGREDIENTS: ⅓ oz. (10 g) dried tomatoes, ⅓ oz. (10 g) dried morels, 7 oz. (200 g) ground chicken breast (skinned), 1 tsp. (4 g) salt (2% of chicken by weight), 2 liters soft water

DIRECTIONS: 1. Immerse dried tomatoes and dried morels in water and refrigerate overnight. 2. Salt the ground chicken breast and set aside for an hour. 3. Add 2 to 1 and simmer until the chicken is sufficiently cooked through. 4. Strain, without skimming, through a cloth.

From tradition to innovation, creating dashi with new ingredients

Is it possible to think up new combinations of ingredients that will trigger umami's synergistic effect, to create a new style of dashi? Here we introduce a new dashi recipe devised by Yoshihiro Murata. Possible even in places where Japanese ingredients such as kombu and katsuobushi are unavailable, this dashi combines umami-rich foods in accordance with general umami principles for preparing Japanese dishes. Inspired by this new dashi, Peruvian chef Pedro Miguel Schiaffino in turn came up with his own original dashi combining dried tomatoes and onions close to native Peruvian varieties, along with *charqui* (dried alpaca meat, a traditional Peruvian preserved food). You don't have to confine yourself to Chef Murata's idea for a new style of dashi; experiment with making your own.

Tackling the challenge of healthy eating

A growing number of chefs are now deliberately moving away from rich butter and cream-based concoctions, in a movement that first emerged with the promotion of nouvelle cuisine, and has gathered pace with chefs championing lighter, water-based "cuisine à l'eau." An increasing number of chefs are turning for inspiration to the techniques of Japanese cuisine.

In Japanese cooking the focus tends to be on appearance, knife skills, and special dishes such as sushi and sashimi, but the feature of Japanese food cuisine most worthy of attention is its healthiness. Take the *kaiseki*-style lunchbox served by Yoshihiro Murata as an example: despite using over forty ingredients, they contain less than 500 kilocalories. This is made possible by the Japanese technique of using the umami of dashi—as opposed to fats such as butter or cream—to draw out flavor.

Recent years have seen an influx to Japan of chefs, not just from France but from all over the globe, to study Japanese cooking techniques. Learning how to prepare dashi, they acquire the skill of utilizing umami as a substitute for fats and oils. Chefs like this are now starting to return to their own regions and incorporate umami into their own cooking.

Kikunoi *kaiseki*-style bento

Foods high in umami

Vegetables

Tomatoes

Ripe, red tomatoes have a sweet, well-rounded taste. This is because as the tomato ripens, the sugar content rises along with the volume of the umami component glutamate. The amount of glutamate also varies between different parts of the tomato. Analysis has revealed that the jelly-like section around the seeds contains about 1.5 times the glutamate of the firm flesh.

Tomatoes are eaten fresh or cooked in sauces and soups. They are also made into condiments such as concentrated tomato paste and tomato ketchup, and other processed products such as dried tomatoes. There is evidence that dried tomatoes have not only a higher glutamate concentration due to reduced moisture, but also have guanylate, which is not found in raw tomatoes, making them more umami-rich than raw tomatoes.

These days tomatoes are a familiar umami food available worldwide, but this widespread use of tomatoes is surprisingly recent. A plant of the Americas, native to Peru, the tomato was unknown in Europe, Asia or Africa until the Spanish conquest of

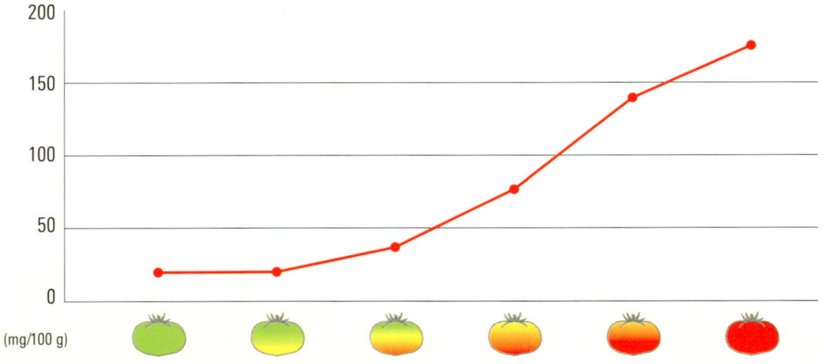

Free gultamate levels at varying stages of tomato ripeness

Mexico in the early sixteenth century. Since then it has been adopted as a major food in the Mediterranean, the Balkans, the Middle East, Asia, in the United States and regions into which U.S. culinary culture has been imported.

The tamarillo: a close umami relative of the tomato

The tamarillo, a tomato-like plant seen in South American markets, is another food high in umami. A member of the eggplant family, the tamarillo is closely related to the tomato, and like the tomato, native to the Andes and surrounding area. Familiar to South Americans for centuries, it was newly identified as an umami food. When the amino acid component was analyzed, 480 mg/100 g of glutamate was detected in the flesh and over 1200 mg/100 g in the jelly-like part around the seeds, revealing the tamarillo to be a superior umami food to the tomato. Such careful resampling of older, familiar foods may well lead to many more exciting new umami food discoveries.

Tamarillo

Other vegetables

Vegetables relatively high in the umami substance glutamate include asparagus, broccoli, Chinese cabbage, carrots, leeks, onions and other members of the allium family and peas. Long before the synergistic effect of umami substances was scientifically proven, Europeans would add vegetables such as carrots and onions to inosinate-rich meat when making soup stock, while in China, cooks used vegetables such as ginger and green onions. Our ancestors knew from practical experience that such combinations would draw out the umami more effectively, resulting in a more appetizing soup.

Many vegetables other than those just mentioned also contain the umami substance glutamate, albeit not in large amounts. The possibilities for devising new ways of using umami are set to grow, whether by taking puréed vegetables or vegetable cooking water, which is generally discarded, and boiling down to concentrate the umami, or boosting umami by capitalizing on the synergistic effect of combining glutamate with foods containing substances like inosinate and guanylate.

Concentrating umami by dehydration

In Japan there is a type of vegetarian cuisine known as *Shojin* cuisine. Based on the dietary regimen of Chinese Zen Buddhism, it became integrated after arriving in Japan with the country's natural ingredients and dietary habits, developing into its current form. In accordance with Buddhist precepts, Shojin cuisine excludes animal products such as meat and fish, as well as strong-smelling ingredients like chives, garlic and onions. Thus, being an animal product, the ichiban-dashi indispensable to Japanese cooking cannot be used.

Instead, Shojin cuisine uses dried vegetables, shiitake mushrooms, soy beans and gourd, or the dried peels of vegetables such as carrots and daikon radishes, combined with kombu dashi. Drying vegetables not only concertrates their glutamate, but also generates the new umami substance guanylate. Recent studies have shown that drying daikon radishes contains small amount of guanylate which is not found in raw daikon. Advanced analytical techniques in recent years have made it possible to identify tiny amounts of guanylate previously

Macambo: an umami food of the Amazon

Yoshihiro Murata

In December 2011 I joined chefs from Peru, Brazil and elsewhere on a three-day cruise along tributaries of the Amazon which was organized by the Umami Information Center, starting from the town of Iquitos in northern Peru. Meals on the cruise were prepared by Peruvian chef Pedro Miguel Schiaffino, who also appears in this book, and thanks in no inconsiderable part to his efforts, the trip turned into a priceless encounter with some unusual foods of the Amazon. At breakfast we were served various Amazonian fruits. Having sampled the cacao-shaped *macambo*, I detected a lingering sensation that I thought was an umami aftertaste. To confirm this, sprinkling a little salt, I found the umami taste even more apparent. For dinner on the final night of the three-day cruise, each of the chefs on board presented an umami dish made from Amazonian ingredients, mine being grilled piranha with macambo sauce. On returning to Japan I was astounded by the results of an amino acid analysis of the fruit. High in glutamate, 220mg/100g, there was no doubt that as I suspected, macambo was an umami fruit.

Macambo

difficult to detect, allowing us to acquire new expertise on the umami substances in vegetables.

Dried shiitake mushrooms are also high in guanylate, which when combined with the glutamate of kombu, enhances umami by the synergistic effect.

Meat

Effect of aging

Meat has been used for millennia to flavor food and as a foundation for taste. The great 19th-century chef Carême declared, "Beef is the soul of cooking." In his day, beef boiled

complete with fat, bones and aromatic herbs, then flavored and strained to remove impurities, formed the most important base for cooking. The liquid from simmered meat is called broth or *bouillon* (the French word meaning boiled). *Glace de viande*, made by reducing umami-rich stock to a paste or jelly, is the ultimate flavor enhancer, the very soul of umami. Today, there is no need to expend such time and effort: instant powders, pastes, and bouillon cubes are available, all containing plenty of umami.

The umami of meat is composed of inosinate and glutamate. Inosinate is not found in the live animal, but is produced posthumously with the breakdown of substances that form the basis of inosinate. Since protein is also broken down into amino acids at the same time, the amount of amino acids such as glutamate also rises after the animal is slaughtered. This is the process known as meat aging. Generally speaking, larger animals age more slowly, with aging time longer for beef than poultry. As aging advances there is a danger of putrefaction, so it is vital to identify when the meat is at its most flavorful peak.

Cured ham

Processed meats such as ham and sausages are also good umami foods. In particular dry-cured hams such as *prosciutto*, *jamon iberico*, and *jamon serrano* are full of umami. Dry-cured ham is made by taking salted pork and hanging it to dry for an extended period in a dry location at low temperature. During this process, glutamate and other amino acids increase thanks to the breakdown of meat proteins, and flavor components become concentrated due to the removal of moisture, thus boosting the

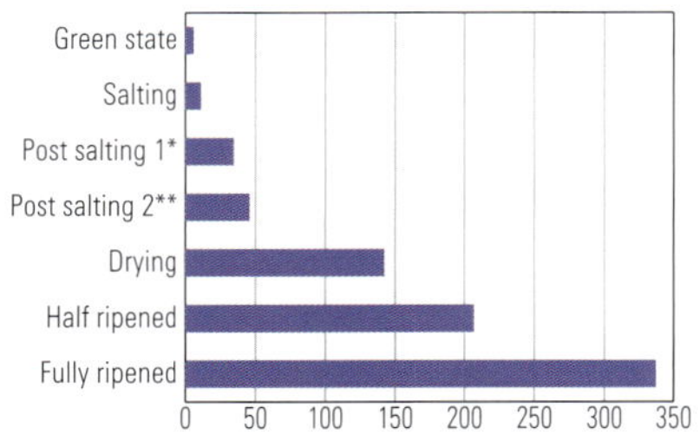

* cool temperature, high humidity, 2 months (winter)
**higher temperature, lower humidity, about 1½ months (spring)

Changes in glutamate content during cured ham ripening

glutamate umami content. Inosinate is found in large amounts in pork prior to processing, but over the long aging period of one to two years, it is broken down by enzyme action until almost none remains. However, the aging of cured ham has the effect of condensing glutamate, which more than compensates for the reduction in inosinate.

China is also home to a variety of ham very similar to the cured hams of Europe: *Xinhua* ham. This is made using pigs with lean flesh, achieved by giving the animals feed containing tea leaves and Chinese cabbage, both fermented. The meat is salted using mineral salt, dried in the sun, then hung in a dry place to ripen. The drying and ripening processes not only boosts the ham's keeping properties, it also concentrates umami and is indispensable to enhancing flavor. The dry-aging process popular in recent years is also grounded in this idea.

Venison aging with multigrain malt—a new method in Japan

With the passing of summer and transition to cooler autumn days comes the season eagerly awaited by lovers of game meat. Though game has not always been a familiar food to the Japanese, in recent years a burgeoning wild deer population has prompted numerous studies on getting the best out of venison. Low in fat and high in iron and protein, venison is being investigated for use as a high-quality protein to help guard against anaemia and poor nutrition in the elderly. It is now known that applying multigrain malt made by yeasting grains such as barley and millet to venison during its comparatively short aging period of 7 to 10 days in order to build up greater amounts of amino acids including glutamate, a delicious venison even richer in flavor can be produced. During the usual aging period of a week or so, glutamate rises from 25 mg/100g to 35 mg/100 g, but the addition of multigrain malt at 5% by weight of the meat greatly increases glutamate up to 280 mg/100 g, as well as making the meat juicier and more tender. Effective new preparations for venison making intelligent use of multigrain malt are under development, and the future is likely to bring wider consumption not only of venison, but other game as well.

Seafood

Seafood can be eaten raw (particularly in Japan) or processed in many ways throughout the world, including drying, salting and fermenting.

Umami from seafood imparts a rich flavor to cooking. In addition to glutamate, seafood contains nucleotide-based umami in the form of substances such as inosinate and adenylate*, which is unique to shellfish such as clams, oysters, scallops and octopus. Depending on the method and duration of preservation, enzymes in the bodies of marine life convert these nucleotides into different non-umami substances. When dealing with fresh seafood, timing is vital for peak flavor.

* Adenylate displays a milder umami than inosinate, but like inosinate, there is a recognized synergistic effect by which it acquires a stronger umami when combined with glutamate.

Katsuobushi (dried bonito) and niboshi (dried anchovy)

Seasonings consisting of dried or fermented seafood are found throughout Asia, including Japan. *Katsuobushi* (dried bonito) and *niboshi* (dried anchovy) are two of the main umami foods in Japanese gastronomy together with kombu. Katsuobushi is the world's hardest and driest food. After boiling, bonito fillets are repeatedly dried and smoked several times. In some cases, mold is allowed to grow on the surface to reduce moisture inside to the absolute minimum. Katsuobushi that has undergone this molding process is called *honkarebushi*, and is highly prized.

The most important umami component of katsuobushi is inosinate, of which it contains 687 mg/100 g. Inosinate in fish is produced when adenosine triphosphate (ATP), a substance contained in the muscles as an energy source, is broken down posthumously by enzymes. However, if this dissolution becomes too advanced, inosinate change to another substance lacking in umami. During katsuobushi manufacture, the fish is first cooked at close to 212°F (100°C). This process deactivates the enzymes that turn inosinate into a different substance, preserving the inosinate produced in the bonito's muscles without further alteration. Repeated drying and smoking to minimize moisture content concentrates the umami and turns the katsuobushi into a long-lasting end product.

Katsuobushi is planed into thin flakes reminiscent of wood shavings for use. The flakes are added to boiling water, removed from heat and allowed to sink, then poured through a straining cloth. The umami is extracted during this process, but boiling too vigorously, or mashing the flakes forcefully through the straining cloth may result in a fishy smell, a bitter or unpleasant taste, or cloudiness in the dashi. Aroma and taste can also vary between different preparations of katsuobushi, depending on where the shavings come from (back or belly flesh, or from both sides of the fish), differences in the manufacturing process, or differences in thickness when shaved.

The main ingredient in niboshi is Japanese anchovy (*Engraulis japonicus*). Niboshi is also made from other fish such as flying fish, saury, trevally, and sea bream. *Ni* means to boil, and *boshi* (or *hoshi*) to dry, and just as in making katsuoboshi, first boiling then drying the fish preserves the inosinate without allowing it to convert into other substances with no umami.

When making dashi from niboshi, it is necessary to remove the head and innards of the fish: not doing so can result in an unpleasant taste, such as excessive "fishiness" or bitterness.

Dried cod

In the Mediterranean, South America, and elsewhere, dried cod is used in cooking. The fish is salted generously and dried, then rehydrated and used as an ingredient and/or flavoring. Cod is deemed to "go off" quickly, and inosinate in cod meat decreases rapidly compared to other fish. Dried cod does not contain inosinate, because unlike katsuobushi and niboshi, the cod is not cooked as part of the preservation process. However salting and drying enhance its keeping qualities, removing all the fish's moisuture and condensing the umami from glutamate.

Dried cod

Dried shrimp and other shellfish

As ingredients with condensed umami, dried shrimp and scallops are also favorites in Asia, Latin America and some African countries. These are usually added directly during cooking, or rehydrated and used in soup. As stated in the section on katsuobushi and niboshi, there is a substance serving as an energy source in the muscles of fish, ATP, that forms the basis of inosinate. Similarly, the nucleotide adenylate is also found before cooking.

Seaweed

Kombu

One of the main ingredients in Japanese dashi is the edible seaweed kombu. When dried, it contains an extraordinarily high concentration of glutamate: approximawtely 1000 to 1600 mg/100 g. Part of the brown algae family, kombu is harvested along Japan's northern coasts, from northernmost Hokkaido extending down to parts of the northeast region of the main island Honshu. The kombu growing along the Japanese coast is fundamentally all of the same variety, but tastes different depending on the area and growing environment. *Ma-kombu*, *Rausu* kombu and *Rishiri* kombu are comparatively fleshy, and are used mainly to make dashi. Varieties such as *Hidaka* kombu and *Naga* kombu are slightly thinner, and are used in simmered dishes or simply eaten as is.

Technique to bring out umami

There are two methods of extracting umami from kombu: *mizudashi* (in cold water) and *nidashi* (boiling). To make using the mizudashi method, wipe the kombu with a well-wrung damp cloth, then immerse in water. Soaking time will vary according to variables such as climate and the quality of the kombu, but generally takes about ten hours at refrigerator temperatures.

In the nidashi method, the usual procedure is to place the kombu in cold water, simmer over a low to medium heat and remove just before the water comes to a boil. Research has shown, however, that with Rishiri kombu, simmering at around 140°F (60°C) for an hour or so allows the maximum umami to be extracted. This method is currently used in some *kaiseki*-style restaurants, mainly in Kyoto. In any case, it is important not to let the kombu boil vigorously at a high temperature, as this can result in a strong seaweed odor, sliminess, or discoloration of other foods.

Kombu will keep for a year if stored in a can or other sealed container, away from high temperatures and humid conditions to prevent it going moldy. Using large amounts of dessicant or storing uncovered in the refrigerator may cause the kombu to not only lose its tempting fragrance, but absorb other odors as well, to detrimental effect. Some kombu has been covered with a white powder: this is not a crystallizing of the glutamate umami component, but a slightly sweet substance called mannitol.

Kombu making process

Water used to make dashi

Water may seem tasteless, yet in reality there are subtle differences in taste between different waters, due to the substances dissolved in them. Hardness is used as a value to indicate the character of water, determined by the volume of calcium and magnesium contained in it. The volume of these minerals is converted to its weight in calcium carbonate and expressed in milligrams per liter to indicate the water's hardness. The World Health Organization defines water with a value under 60 as soft, and over 180 as hard.

Water in Japan is on the soft side at a hardness of 20 to 80 or so. Because soft water contains few minerals, it has no marked taste, making it suitable for simple Japanese dashi as a pure umami extract. Conversely, hard water having a high mineral content in of itself is suitable for making the stock used in western cooking, because it stops unpleasant and unwanted flavors from meat and fish leaching into the liquid. Thus both Japanese dashi and western stock are best prepared using water from their respective regions.

Making *kombu-jime*

A popular method of utilizing the umami in kombu is *kombu-jime*. Raw white fish fillet such as amberjack, sea bream or flounder is wrapped in kombu moistened with sake and refrigerated for a few hours. This transfers umami from the kombu to the fillet, and moisture from the fish to the kombu, thus achieving a different taste and texture from the original white fish fillet. Kombu-jime has actually been found to increase the volume of glutamate in the flesh of fish.

Kombu-jime

Wakame and nori

In Japan and Korea, in addition to kombu, seaweeds such as *wakame* and *nori* have long been favorite foods. Wakame is distributed along most of the Japanese coastline from southern Hokkaido on south. Most wakame is preserved in some way, either dried or salted, and is rehydrated before use as an ingredient in dishes such as soups and salads. Wakame does contain glutamate, but only in small amounts compared to kombu.

Nori is seaweed dried in sheets, and is well known for its use in sushi. Nori is rich in amino acids, starting with glutamate. Sheet nori is highly recommended as an easy way to include umami in the diet. Nori also contains the umami substance guanylate.

Other seaweeds

There are only a limited number of places worldwide where seaweed is consumed as a matter of choice, Japan being one of the main ones, but seaweeds such as *dulse*, gathered on the coasts of Europe and North America, are also used by some for food. In South America seaweeds such as *cochayuyo* and *cushuro* (actually a blue-green bacteria colony that resembles seaweed) are dried for eating. These seaweeds are high in glutamate and other amino acids.

Cochayuyo

Mushrooms

Fresh mushrooms are generally high in glutamate. That is why various kinds of fresh mushrooms are often used in cooking: along with their unique texture and aroma they enhance flavor through umami. Mushrooms are also often dried. The primary reason to dry mushrooms was preservation, to keep their tissues intact. But drying has another effect on mushrooms: it facilitates the production of yet a different umami component, guanylate, which is not found in fresh mushrooms.

Mushrooms are classified in the kingdom of fungi, which is separate from plants, and contain a high amount of RNA (ribonucleic acid) inside their cells. Guanylate is a nucleotide and one of the building blocks of RNA.

During the process of dehydration, the membranes of cells from the tissue of mushrooms tears and RNA is usually broken down into guanylate by the effect of an enzyme called nuclease. The reaction does not proceed further without the presence of water. The first step to promote this reaction is to keep dried mushrooms in cold water, not in hot water which damages tissues, for at least 7 or 8 hours. Next, it is necessary to cook the mushrooms in the same water. The optimum temperature to activate the nuclease enzyme is between 140 and 160°F (60 and 70°C). This means that rehydration and temperature are important to obtain a guanylate-rich dashi from dried mushrooms. There is another enzyme which converts

Rehydrating shiitake

guanylate into a different substance with no umami taste. This enzyme is activated at 85 and 105°F (30 to 40°C). This is why it is necessary to quickly heat the water to 140 and 160°F (60 to 70°C) when making dashi from dried mushrooms, this promotes the production of the umami substance guanylate. Since the glutamate in fresh mushrooms is preserved during the drying process, at the end, dashi made from dried mushrooms has a strong umami taste due to the synergism between glutamate and guanylate.

Traditional fermented foods

Fermented products made from protein-rich foods like meat, fish, grains and beans are full of umami from glutamate. There are fermented products with umami from all over the world.

Chi and jiang

In East Asia traditional seasonings and condiments made by fermenting grains, beans, small fish and shrimp have been used since ancient times to add salt and umami to cooking. For many centuries the Chinese have used a fermented food known as *douchi*

Dobanjiang

Tianmianjiang

or *chi*, made from small, semi-dried black soy beans. Douchi is eaten as is, or used as a condiment in conjunction with garlic or other aromatics. Similar fermented products can be found in other parts of East Asia.

Another fermented food called *jiang* is also used to flavor cooking on a day-to-day basis. In ancient times jiang was made by fermenting finely-chopped meat or fish with salt and yeast in a sealed container. The jiang varieties used commonly these days, such as *dobanjiang* and *tianmianjiang,* are made from beans and grains, and have been around since about the first century BCE. These seasonings have complex, seductive flavors combining umami, salt, various amino acids and aromatics, and when used in cooking impart a unique depth.

Anchovies

Food consisting of fermented fish is not exclusive to Southeast Asian cuisines, but is familiar to Europeans too, in the form of anchovies. Likely a legacy of the fish sauces *garum* and *liquamen* loved by the ancient Romans, anchovies are fermented almost the same way as in Southeast Asian fish sauces. A favorite since the earliest times in places such as Italy and southern France, anchovies are extremely high in glutamate, and are used whole or as a paste in many dishes. Anchovies are found in cooking the world over, flavoring meat and vegetable dishes, pasta in Italy and noodles in Asia, on pizzas and hors d'oeuvres, and in dressings.

Anchovies

Products like douchi and jiang originating in China were developed into fermented condiments such as soy sauce and miso familiar throughout East Asia. Soy sauce and miso are also high in glutamate, and today remain favorite ways to add umami, saltiness, and uniquely regional flavors to cuisine.

There are many different fermented foods and condiments other than chi, jiang, fish sauces and anchovies. Almost without exception, they contain umami from gultamate. The fermented foods of your own local culture that you use without even thinking may well be giving your cooking not only its familiar flavor, but umami as well.

Cheese

Cheese is a major umami food in the west. Enzymes, mold, and bacteria are added to cow's, sheep's or goat's milk, which is fermented and matured, or further treated for a longer shelf life, to make cheese. During the fermentation and maturation processes, milk proteins break down into amino acids. Glutamate is the most abundant among these amino acids. Umami is higher in hard cheeses such as cheddar and Emmental, which have longer aging times. Younger cheeses with a high water content, and other fermented dairy products such as yogurt and sour cream, have minimal glutamate compared to well-aged cheeses.

Parmigiano-Reggiano is an aged cheese originating in the Parma region of Italy. When Parmigiano-Reggiano is aged for over two years, it contains an incredible 1200 to 1600 mg of glutamate per 100 g, making it the king of umami foods. During this extended maturation

Parmesan cheese

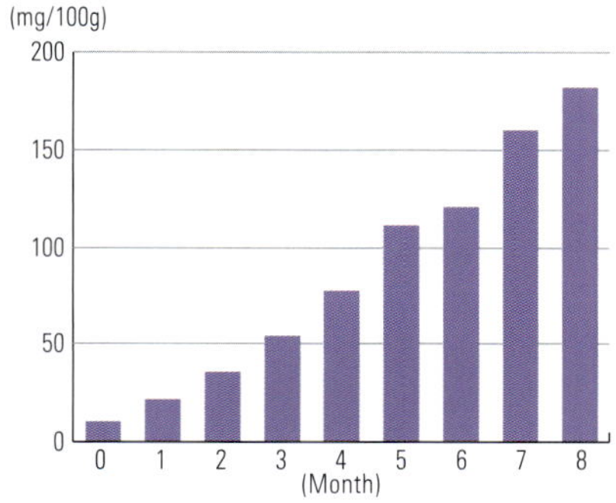

Free glutamate levels of cheddar cheese aging

period, glutamate is produced, while at the same time moisture evaporation concentrates components in the cheese, imparting a strong umami taste. Well-aged Parmigiano-Reggiano is coated in irregular white crystals. These granules are often mistaken for glutamate, but when removed and analyzed in isolation, they have been found to be formed by the concentration of various amino acids other than glutamate that have low solubility in water, mainly *valine*, *leucine* and *isoleucine*.

Teas

Green tea leaves are high in amino acids including glutamate and *theanine*, which displays low levels of umami and sweetness. Most of the black teas and oolong teas distributed widely throughout the world are what are known as fermented teas. In order to color the leaves and the tea itself brown and produce a unique depth of flavor and aroma, these teas

Green tea

are made by triggering the enzyme *oxidase* in the tea leaves under humid conditions. Because this fermentation process alters the amino acids such as glutamate in the leaves, fermented teas do not contain umami. Green tea on the other hand is a non-fermented tea, made by steaming the leaves without allowing enzymatic oxidation. This means that the glutamate and theanine in the tea leaves are preserved along with the umami.

There are not that many different cultivars of the tea used in green tea, and the same ones are employed as for black tea and oolong tea, but there are various types and grades according to the method of cultivation, the selection of leaves to pick and the method of manufacture. The premium Japanese tea *gyokuro*, rich in theanine and glutamate, contains approximately 2500 mg of theanine and 450 mg of glutamate in every 100 g, around 100 times the theanine and twenty-five times the glutamate of everyday *hojicha* (roasted green tea). Gyokuro is made from just the first new shoots of tea bushes grown under cover. The covering is to prevent sunlight causing the amino acid theanine to turn into *catechins*, which impart an astringent taste.

In Japan the various taste characteristics of each green tea are utilized in different ways, by drinking gyokuro when the aim is to savor the tea itself alongside traditional confections, and drinking hojicha to refresh the palate after a meal. Powdered green tea, *matcha*, is also used in cooking and confections to impart flavor and color.

Training yourself to identify umami

The quickest way to master the use of umami is to experience umami and understand its properties. Start by sampling umami-rich foods, physically sensing the characteristics of umami for yourself. In order to detect subtle umami in food, it is important to keep the inside of the mouth clean. Make sure to have water on hand to rinse your tongue. Before and during tasting, also avoid partaking of anything with a strong flavor and/or aroma such as coffee or tobacco.

Can you describe the different tastes while chewing tomatoes?

Do you feel any sensations after eating tomatoes? You may not be able to explain the sensations on your tongue.

Do you feel a coating sensation on your tongue?

This ambiguous and subtle taste on your tongue is umami.

Tasting using cherry tomatoes

Tomatoes are rich in umami. Bite-size cherry tomatoes especially are perfect when first acquiring an understanding of umami. To begin, remove the stem and pop the tomato in your mouth. Chew it about thirty times, taking your time to sense the changing taste on your tongue. First you will probably detect sour and sweet tastes, along with the distinctive grassy aroma of tomatoes. After chewing thirty times, do you notice a faint taste lingering on your tongue? That taste is umami. The umami component of cherry tomatoes is glutamate. You will probably feel yourself continuing to produce saliva even after swallowing the tomato. As mentioned earlier, umami promotes salivation. The same experience can be obtained using dried tomato or salt-free tomato paste.

Tasting using cheese

With cheese, it is not fresh cheeses with a high moisture content that are rich in umami, but hard cheeses such as aged cheddars, Comté, and Mimolette. Italy's extra-hard Parmigiano-Reggiano contains so much glutamate that it almost seems like solid umami. Slice cheese very thinly and place a piece about fingertip-size on the center of your tongue.

First to emerge will be strong salt and cheese flavors, but as you slowly chew and the cheese dissolves in your mouth, those flavors will subside, eventually leaving just a faint taste on the tongue. This taste is umami. The longer a cheese is aged, the more intense the umami, due to breakdown of protein in the cheese into glutamate and other amino acids. We recommend sampling cheeses with different aging times to compare them.

Tasting using cured ham

Choose an unsmoked dry-cured ham, such as Italian prosciutto or Spanish jamon serrano, made by salting pork and aging it for one or two years. Smoked hams have too intense an aroma, which can make it difficult to identify umami. Because dry-cured hams are very salty, take a small, thin piece and place it on your tongue then carefully chew it. When the saltiness has gone, you should be able to detect a unique taste on your tongue. This is umami.

Tasting using Japanese dashi

Prepare kombu dashi for its glutamate, katsuo dashi (made from bonito flakes) for inosinate, or dashi from dried shiitake mushrooms rich in guanylate. Start by tasting each carefully to detect the characteristics of umami from glutamate, inosinate or guanylate respectively. Next, to understand the synergistic effect of combining glutamate with inosinate or guanylate, mix the different dashi types. Tasting the mixture of dashi, you may feel a stronger umami than the each type of dashi. This is the synergistic effect.

Tasting using vegetable soup—the role of umami in cooking

Preparation of vegetable soup for the tasting

As mentioned earlier, vegetables contain glutamate. If simmered slowly over a long period, ample umami is extracted from vegetables, but a short cooking time leads to insufficient umami extraction. Moreover, the taste and aroma of the ingredients do not seem to be harmonized when cooked too briefly. To learn about the role of umami in cooking and the synergistic effect of umami, let us start by preparing a vegetable soup below that is deliberately undercooked.

To understand the role of umami in cooking

Adding monosodium glutamate (MSG)—crystals of the purest umami—to the undercooked soup

Vegetable soup

INGREDIENTS: 4 cups (1 L) water, 1⅓ oz. (40 g) broccoli stalks, 1⅓ oz. (40 g) celery stalks, 1⅓ oz. (40 g) mushrooms, ½ oz. (15 g) onion, ½ oz. (15 g) carrot, ⅙ oz. (5 g) parsley stalks, salt 0.3% of soup weight

DIRECTIONS: Cut all the vegetables into ½ in. (1 cm) cubes. Add to the water, place over low heat and cook for 20 minutes at 175 to 185°F (80 to 85°C). Do not allow to come to a boil. Place a straining cloth or paper towel in a sieve and strain the liquid. Measure the broth after vegetables have been removed and season with salt equal to 0.3% of weight. These ingredients and instructions will make around 3⅓ cups (800 ml). This vegetable soup can be used for the tasting for understanding the synergistic effect of umami and the role of umami in cooking.

*Please use only the stems of broccoli, celery and parsley since the remaining parts have a strong flavor and impart a bitter taste to the soup.

will help you to understand the role of umami in cooking, in an easy experiment you can conduct in your own kitchen.

Preparation: First, keep a part of the vegetable soup already mentioned before. And then prepare another portion with 0.1% to 0.2% MSG by weight.

Tasting: You will probably find the flavors of the ingredients in the broth without MSG to be somehow dispersed, giving an unbalanced impression. Next, try the broth with the MSG is added. The taste should be more balanced. By comparing the undercooked broth to the broth with added MSG, you will understand just how much umami contributes to improve the compatibility of different tastes.

To detect the synergetic effect of umami

Preparation: Take 2⅔ oz. (80 g) of ground chicken breast, add to one of the 1⅔ cups (400 ml) vegetable soup described before and stir thoroughly. Cook on a moderate to low flame without skimming, then strain.
Tasting: First, sample the broth without the chicken. Then sample the broth with chicken added.
The inosinate from the chicken and glutamate extracted from the vegetables synergistically enhance umami, which will enable you to detect the umami more intensely.

For more information about umami, please visit the website of the Umami Information Center: http://www.umamiinfo.com/)

S. Yamaguchi and K. Ninomiya et al., Food Rev. Intl., 1998. **14** (2&3)

Contents of umami substances

Glutamate

Vegetables	(mg/100 g)
Tamarillo	470–1200
Tomato	150–250
Macambo	220
Green pea	110
Garlic	100
Potato	30–100
Chinese cabbage	40–90
Soy bean	70–80
Daikon (Dried)	200
Carrot	40–80
Beet	60
Green asparagus	50
White asparagus	40
Onion	20–50
Scallions (Green onion)	20–50
Broccoli	30
Celery	20–30
Ginger	20
Meat and egg	(mg/100 g)
Chicken	40
Beef	30
Pork	20
Venison	25–35
Aged cured ham	340
Egg yolk	50
Egg (Whole)	20
Seafoods	(mg/100 g)
Scallop	140
Kuruma shrimp	120

Sea urchin	100
Short necked clam	90
Crab	20–80
Octopus	20
Niboshi (Dried sardine)	40–50
Katsuobushi (Dried bonito)	30–40
Dried cod	10
Seaweeds	(mg/100 g)
Kombu	1200–3400
Nori	1380
Cochayuyo	100
Mushrooms	(mg/100 g)
[FRESH]	
Honshimeji	140
Enoki	90
Shiitake	70
Mushroom	40
[DRIED]	
Shiitake	1060
Morel	310
Oyster mushroom	310
Porcini	80
Traditional foods	(mg/100 g)
Fermented bean products (other than soy sauce and miso)	140–1700
Anchovies	630–1440
Cheese	300–1680
Fish sauce	620–1380
Soy sauce	410–1260
Green tea	220–670
Miso	90–210

Inosinate

Meat and poultry	(mg/100 g)
Pork	230
Chicken	230
Beef	80
Seafoods	(mg/100 g)
Yellowtail	410–470
Sardine	420
Sea bream	180–400
Bonito (fresh)	130–400
Tuna	250–360
Mackerel	160–290
Cod	130–290
Kuruma shrimp	90
Niboshi (Dried sardine)	350–800
Katsuobushi (Dried bonito)	470–700

Guanylate

	(mg/100 g)
Shiitake (dried)	150
Enoki (cooked)	50
Morel (dried)	40
Scallop	10
Nori	10
Dried tomato	10
Porcini (dried)	10
Oyster mushroom (dried)	10

G L O S S A R Y

A

Agar powder
Thickening agent extracted from various seaweeds (algae) and usually sold as a white or semi-translucent powder. Agar can be substituted with *kanten* powder, also made from algae.

Aji amarillo
Capsicum baccatum, a long, thin Peruvian pepper colored yellow verging on orange. Medium-hot, with a pleasantly fruity flavor.

Aji dulce
Capsicum chinense, small, light green pepper that turns red if left long enough on the plant. Related to the habañero, but with a much milder, smoky flavor.

Aji rocoto
Capsicum pubescens, a plump red Peruvian pepper, meaty and very hot.

B

Black cod
Anoplopoma fimbria, a dark-colored marine fish of North American Pacific waters, not actually related to cod, with rich but mild off-white flesh.

Brown rice
Rice that has only been husked, leaving the surface bran intact. Contains vitamin B1 and other nutrients not found in polished (white) rice.

C

Causa
Peruvian mashed potatoes. Basically mixed with key lime, onion, chili and oil.

Ceviche
Dish consisting of raw seafood marinated in lime or lemon juice, olive oil, herbs and spices. Popular in Latin America.

Cochayuyo
Seaweed that has been eaten mainly in South America for over 10,000 years. High in glutamate and other amino acids.

Cushuro
Seaweed-like blue-green cyanobacteria colony found in the Andean highlands. Traditionally, mainly eaten among Andean hill tribes. High in glutamate and other amino acids.

D

Daikon
Long, large white radish. Milder than the Western radish, can also be eaten raw. Grated daikon is often served with dishes to aid digestion.

Dashi
Japanese stock often made of dried bonito flakes and kombu.

Dulce de leche
Sweetened condensed milk prepared by slowly heating to create a product that derives its taste from the Maillard reaction, changing flavor and color.

E

Ebi taro
Variety of taro root originating in parts of western Japan such as Kyoto and Osaka. Named for its resemblance to shrimp (*ebi*), it has fine-grained flesh and a creamy texture when cooked.

Edamame
Young, green soybeans, boiled in the pod and used in various dishes. Edamame are at their best in summer, but available frozen all year round.

F

Flounder
Pseudopleuronectes americanus, a flatfish, with its eyes on the right side of its body.

Furikake
Food made by taking powdered fish, adding nori, katsuobushi, sesame and spices, processing into granules and drying. Used as a topping on rice.

G

Ginkgo
Nut from the gingko tree, known in Japan as *ginnan*. Grilled as is, or used in steamed dishes.

Gobo (burdock root)
A long root vegetable, *Arctium lappa*, earthy in flavor. When cooked, it remains pleasantly crunchy. To remove harshness, soak in cold water for a while before cooking.

H

Hijiki
Black string-shaped seaweed harvested in Japan, China and Korea. Sold blanched and dried. Rehydrate by soaking in plenty of water.

Honkarebushi
Variety of katsuobushi made by repeatedly applying mold in the katsuobushi production process to eliminate moisture during maturation. Molding boosts both umami and the distinctive bonito aroma.

I

Ise lobster
Large lobster viewed as a luxury food in Japan and often served on special occasions. Can be cooked or eaten raw as sashimi.

J

Japanese cucumber
Small, long cucumber with a thin, edible skin, highly regarded for its crunchiness.

Japanese eggplant
Small, long eggplant with a thin skin and delicate flavor.

K

Kabocha
A Japanese winter squash. *Kabocha* has a dark green skin and bright orange flesh. Popular for its sweet, buttery flavor and fluffy texture when cooked.

Katsuobushi
Katsuo (bonito) formed into a boat shape known as a *fushi* for processing. Dried bonito flakes are frequently mixed with kombu to make dashi.

Kiwicha (amaranth)
Amaranth seeds. Amaranth is native to the Andes and Amazon regions. Highly nutritious.

Kombu-jime
Technique used to transfer the umami of kombu to foods such as white fish and vegetables (*see* p.147). Ingredients are sandwiched between pieces of kombu.

Koji
Made by propagating *koji* mold spores on crops such as rice, wheat or soy beans. Indispensable to fermented foods, such as in the production of miso and sake.

Kombu
The seaweed *Laminaria japonica*. High in glutamate, used to make various sorts of dashi in Japanese cuisine.

Kudzu
A thickening starch made from *kudzu* root, often used in Japanese cuisine. Kudzu starch doesn't alter the flavor or color of the food.

L

Leche de tigre
The milky-white,umami-rich liquid left over from marinating ceviche. Can be made in a pinch by puréeing raw fish with citrus juice and spices, then straining the purée.

M

Maca
Lepidium meyenii, a brassica native to the Andes. Cultivated for food since Incan times, the roots are used as a medicinal herb.

Matcha
Tea bushes are shaded for a fortnight or so prior to harvest, and the shoots thus cultivated away from direct sunlight steamed, dried without rolling, and processed into a powder not only drunk as green tea, but used in cooking and confectionery to impart a distinctive flavor. Matcha that is sweeter and less astringent or bitter is preferred and sells for a higher price.

Matsutake
Tricholoma matsutake, a mushroom that grows on the ground in pine forests. With its distinctive aroma, matsutake is Japan's premium mushroom.

Mirin
Sweet rice wine made by adding rice *koji* and brewing alcohol to steamed sticky rice and fermenting. Stops ingredients from disintegrating during cooking, and adds sweetness.

Miso
A fermented paste made of soybeans, rice and salt. One of the most important seasonings in Japanese cooking.

Myoga
The bud of a plant closely related to ginger. Firmer than ginger, with an intense aroma. Popular finely chopped and used as a condiment in cooking, or pickled in sweet vinegar.

N

Naganegi
Allium fistulosum, a long, thick green onion native to China and Asia. Similar to the leek, the white part is often finely chopped and served raw as a condiment. The tough green tips are used in soups and other dishes.

Niboshi
Small fish simmered and dried, used mainly for making dashi. Frequently made from sardines or pilchards.

Nihaizu
A mixed vinegar made by combining equal amounts of rice vinegar and soy sauce. Used as a base for dressings and marinades.

Nori
Seaweed sheet made from pressed, dried and toasted algae. Regular *nori* sheets are large squares that can be cut into smaller pieces.

Nuka
Rice bran. Highly nutritious, used for making *nukazuke*, a type of pickle. (*see* Rice bran)

O

Oca
Oxalis tuberosa, a yam cultivated on the Andean plateau. Drying makes it sweeter.

P

Paiche
Arapaima gigas, giant freshwater fish of the Amazon. Some specimens grow to over three meters in length. Soft, white flesh makes paiche a popular dish in Latin America.

Panko
Japanese prepared breadcrumbs, available at many food markets.

Ponzu
Japanese citrus-flavored sauce made using citrons or sudachi.

R

Red miso
A miso made from fermented soybeans with little or no rice. Colored a dark brown by the process of steaming the soybeans and long maturation. Generally very salty.

Rice bran
The skin of the rice kernel, a byproduct of polishing brown rice into white. Used to make pickles and for absorbing harshness when boiling bamboo shoots. (*see* Nuka)

Rice vinegar
Brewed vinegar made from rice. Distinguished by its full-bodied taste and mild fragrance, it is suited to dishes that utilize the taste of vinegar such as sushi and *sunomono* (vinegared salads).

S

Saikyo miso
A sweet, white miso from Kyoto, fermented with more than twice as much rice as soybeans.

Sake
A liquor brewed from rice. A popular beverage also used in Japanese cooking.

Sansho
Combines the sharpness of pepper and a tingling sensation that lingers on the tongue. The young leaves are known as *kinome* and are used as an accompaniment to add aroma to various dishes.

Sencha
The term for ordinary Japanese green tea. Generally brewed for 1 to 2 minutes in water of around 70°C (160°F) before drinking.

Shiitake
Mushroom consumed widely in Asia. In Japan, the most popular mushroom of all. *Donko* shiitake, which grow slowly during the cold months, are fat and juicy with intense flavor. Drying concentrates the umami.

Shinjo
Dish made by grinding seafood, adding yamaimo, egg whites and dashi, and then steaming, boiling or frying.

Shiokombu(salt kombu)
Kombu cubed and finely chopped, simmered in a liquid seasoning of salt and soy sauce then dried. Eaten with white rice, or used to flavor cooking.

Shiroita kombu
What remains after kombu has been steeped in vinegar to soften it, and the front and back of the kombu used. The front and back are used in dishes such as tororo kombu. Used mainly to marinate mackerel. Finely chopped, is known as battera kombu.

Shiso
A green or red leafy herb, *Perilla frutescens*, with a refreshing taste.

Soba
Japanese noodles made from buckwheat groats (seeds). Dipped in sauce to eat, commonly served both hot and chilled.

Soy sauce salt
A ready-made flavored seasoning salt made from soy sauce, salt, and starch mixed together and freeze-dried into a powder.

Sudachi
A kind of citrus fruit, *Citrus sudachi*. Harvested when the skin is green, turns yellow as it ripens. Very tart, the juice is served with grilled fish, sashimi. The finely-chopped skin is used as a condiment.

T

Takiawase
Dish made by simmering multiple ingredients such as vegetables, fish and meat separately in a subtle dashi to make the most of the authentic taste of each, then serving together.

Tamari soy sauce
Type of soy sauce made almost entirely from soybeans. High in umami, tamari is thick and rich, with an intense aroma. Heated, it takes on a reddish hue, adding a gloss to cooking.

Tiradito
A Peruvian dish consisting of slices of raw fish dressed with ceviche seasonings.

Tobiko
Salted roe of flying fish. The clumps of tiny golden eggs measuring about 1 mm across are used mainly in sushi.

Tofu
Made by adding the coagulant *nigari* to soy milk to set it. Eaten across Asia. Japanese tofu is characterized by its whiteness and soft texture.

Tororo kombu
Kombu steeped in vinegar to soften, then shaved into threads. Can be eaten raw or as a topping.

Tosaka
Type of seaweed. There are red, green and white varieties, with red *tosaka* turning an even more vibrant red when dried. Often served in salads or with sashimi.

Tumbo
Passiflora quadrangularis, a fruit native to Central and South America. Similar to passionfruit but much larger, with the perfect blend of tartness and sweetness.

U

Umami
One of the five basic tastes along with sweet, sour, salt and bitter. The basic tastes are unique tastes that cannot be produced by mixing other tastes.

Umeboshi
Plums (*Prunus mume*) salted, then sundried. A type of pickle.

Usukuchi soy sauce
The soy sauce used predominantly in the western region in Japan. Though lighter in color than normal soy sauce, it contains more salt. Because it does not tint soups or sauces, is suitable when a dish lighter in color is desired.

W

Wakame
Type of seaweed found in Japan and Korea. Used mainly in miso soup and vinegared salads.

Wasabi
A green horseradish, *Wasabia japonica*, which adds a refreshing and clean taste. Served as an accompaniment to raw fish.

White miso
Miso made with briefly fermented soybeans. Light brown in color and quite sweet.

Y

Yamatoimo
A yam with a slimy, sticky texture. Can be roasted, boiled, or grilled, but is usually grated to enhance its sliminess.

Yuba
The skin that forms on the surface of soy milk when heated. Available both fresh and dried. Rich in botanical proteins.

Yuzu
Japanese citron. Green in summer, turning yellow in winter. Very tart, with a delicate fragrance. Used to add a distinctive sour, citrusy taste to dishes.

CONVERSIONS

Standard U.S. measures are used in this book; the metric conversions in parentheses are also in accordance with U.S. standards.

1 cup = 240 ml (rounded up from 236.59 ml)
1 ounce = 30 g (rounded up from 28.349 g)

Please see the conversion table below as a guide.

Volume

Metric	USA
5 ml	1 teaspoon
15 ml	1 tablespoon
50 ml	3 tablespoons + 1 teaspoon
60 ml	¼ U.S. cup
80 ml	⅓ U.S. cup
100 ml	⅓ U.S. cup + 4 teaspoons
240 ml	U.S. 1 cup
400 ml	U.S. 1⅔ cups
480 ml	U.S. 2 cups = 1 pint
1000 ml (1 L)	U.S. 4 cups = 2 pints = 1 quart

Weight

Grams	USA
10 g	⅓ ounce
15 g	½ ounce
20 g	⅔ ounce
30 g	1 ounce
50 g	1⅔ ounces
100 g	3½ ounces
150 g	5 ounces
200 g	7 ounces

Length

Metric	USA
3 mm	⅛ inch
6 mm	¼ inch
1.25 cm	½ inch
2.5 cm	1 inch
5 cm	2 inches
6.25 cm	2½ inches
7.5 cm	3 inches
10 cm	4 inches

Temperature

Celsius (°C)	Fahrenheit (°F)
120°C	250°F
130°C	275°F
150°C	300°F
160°C	325°F
170°C	340°F
180°C	350°F
190°C	375°F
200°C	390°F

I N D E X

RESTAURANT LIST

THE FAT DUCK
High Street, Bray, Berkshire,
SL6 2AQ, UK
TEL +44 1628 580333
http://www.thefatduck.co.uk/

SaQuaNa
22 place Hamelin, 14600 Honfleur, France
TEL +33 2 31 89 40 80
http://www.alexandre-bourdas.com/

GRAMERCY TAVERN
42 E 20th St, New York, NY 10003, USA
TEL +1 212 477 0777
http://www.gramercytavern.com/

MANRESA
320 Village Lane, Los Gatos,
CA 95030, USA
TEL +1 408 354 4330
http://www.manresarestaurant.com/

CENTRAL
Ca. Santa Isabel 376, Miraflores,
Lima, Peru
TEL +51 1 242 8515
http://centralrestaurante.com.pe/

MALABAR
Camino Real 101, San Isidro,
Lima, Peru
TEL +51 1 440 5200
http://malabar.com.pe/

KIKUNOI
459 shimokawara-cho, Yasakatoriimae-sagaru, Shimokawara-dori,
Higashiyama-ku, Kyoto-shi, Kyoto, Japan
TEL +81 75 561 0015
http://kikunoi.jp/english/

NOBU TOKYO
1st Floor, Toranomon Tower Office, 4-1-28
Toranomon, Minato-ku, Tokyo, Japan
TEL +81 3 5733 0070
http://www.nobutokyo.com/e_index.php

NOBU LONDON
1st Floor, The Metropolitan Hotel,
19 Old Park Lane, London W1K 1LB, UK
TEL +44 207 447 4747
http://www.noburestaurants.com/london/experience/introduction/

*information above is accurate as of February 2014

PRODUCER: Masayuki Uchiyama Dai-Ichi Tsusinsha
PROJECT COORDINATION: Kumiko Ninomiya Umami Information Center
PHOTOGRAPHS: Akira Saito
ART DIRECTION AND DESIGN: Kazuhiko Miki, Miyoko Hayashi Ampersand works
EDITING: Junko Kawakami LETRAS
TRANSLATION: Kirsten McIvor (text), Jeremy Whipple TRY (text), Noriko Yokota (recipes)
COPYEDITING: Derek Wilcox
INTERVIEW WITH HESTON BLUMENTHAL: Mike Loughran
PROOFREADING: Mutsumi Ochi

UMAMI The Fifth Taste 2014年5月23日 初版第1刷発行
著者：うま味インフォメーションセンター／撮影者：齋藤 明／編集者：株式会社第一通信社
発行者 日本出版貿易株式会社 〒101-0064 東京都千代田区猿楽町 1-2-1 電話 03-3292-3751
ISBN 978-4-88996-391-5
印刷・製本 大日本印刷株式会社